THE TRAUMA-INFORMED WRITER

Crafting Authentic Trauma in Genre Fiction

Dr Alicia Leigh

G
P

The Trauma-Informed Writer
Edited by: Emily Halloran
Proofread by: Alicia Leigh and Sarah Newton-John
Formatted by: Alicia Leigh and Rack & Rune Publishing
rackandrune.com
Cover Design by: Graham Davidson

© 2025 Dr Alicia Leigh/Dr Alicia Kindleysides, Australia
www.yourromancebookdoctor.com
www.fallinlovewithleigh.com

Print: ISBN: 978-1-76109-921-2
Ebook: ISBN: 978-1-76109-922-9

First published 2025 by
GINNINDERRA PRESS
PO Box 2 Bentleigh 3204
ginninderrapress.com.au

More books by
A.K. Leigh/Leigh Hatchmann/Alicia Leigh

The Smithfield Series – A.K. Leigh
(Post-Trauma Romance/Trauma Romance/Romantic Suspense)
See Her Run
Crave Her Touch
Trust Her Heart

The Farris Triplets Series – A.K. Leigh
(Crime Romance)
Triple Threat
Triple Terror
Triple Trouble

The Easter in Hallston series – A.K. Leigh
(Contemporary Inspired romance)
Easter Love Connection
Easter Love Match
Easter Love Reunion

The Bloodworth Family Series – Leigh Hatchmann
(Paranormal Romance)
Vengeance of the Witch
Curse of the Witch
Sister of the Witch
Brother of the Witch

Standalone books – A.K. Leigh
To Catch A Christmas Thief *(Christmas Romance/Romantic Suspense)*
The Venus Cure *(Romantic Suspense)*
The Million Dollar Secret *(Contemporary Romance)*
Rescuing Dr. Burgess *(Contemporary Romance)*
The Love Healer *(Post-Trauma Romance)*

Standalone books – Leigh Hatchmann
A Time to Love *(Time Travel Romance)*
Beautiful *(Fairy Tale Romance Retelling)*

Collections, box sets, and anthologies – A.K. Leigh
A Little Bit of Love: Short Story Romance Collection
The Smithfield Series Box Set
A Splash of Romance Anthology

Non-fiction – Alicia Leigh
The Dreaming Writer
The Romance Novel Formula

Find A.K. Leigh/Leigh Hatchmann/Alicia Leigh Online

Websites
www.yourromancebookdoctor.com
www.fallinlovewithleigh.com
YouTube
www.youtube.com/@akleighauthor
Instagram
www.instagram.com/akleighauthor
LinkedIn
www.linkedin.com/in/akleighauthor/
Amazon
www.amazon.com/author/akleigh

List of Tables and Figures

Tables

Figures

Contents

Chapter 1 – Setting The Scene

What is a Trauma-Informed Writer?

Put simply, a trauma-informed writer is a writer who understands the basics of trauma and applies this understanding to their writing in a sensitive way. *The Trauma-Informed Writer* can guide you on your journey to understanding trauma and writing more authentic, sensitive, and accurate representations of trauma, trauma response, post-trauma effects, and trauma recovery. Although this book is primarily aimed at fiction writers (regardless of genre, level of experience, and stage of manuscript), there is plenty of information for other professionals, such as nurses, mental health care practitioners, teachers, students, researchers, and learning and curriculum designers who want to be more trauma-informed in their written communications, essays, articles, or theses.

The Trauma-Informed Writer discusses what constitutes trauma, how to write trauma, the nine major responses to trauma, the major post-trauma effects, and multiple techniques for trauma recovery (in the immediate aftermath of the trauma, in the short-term, and in the long-term). As you read through the following chapters, keep in mind that there is currently <u>no</u> definitive, undebated approach to trauma representation in literature — just like there is still no all-encompassing trauma theory. Nobody has all the answers. Therefore, this book outlines the methods, practices, and theories discovered and applied during my PhD research.

How You Can Become a Trauma-Informed Writer

Before attempting to write sensitive, accurate, and authentic trauma elements, trauma-informed writers need to possess basic knowledge of:
- ways to limit trauma triggers
- the conventions/expectations of their main fiction genre (such as: the tropes, arcs, acts, beats, characters, plot devices, and so forth)
- the intersection of the trauma genre with their main fiction genre (and how this forms a unique trauma-themed subgenre)

- the character, trauma, and relationship arcs
- the definition of trauma
- initial trauma responses (and the traumatised brain)
- the variety of post-trauma effects
- trauma's impact on relationships (regardless of genre, most stories involve interactions between characters)
- therapeutic options
- techniques for triggered individuals (short-term therapy tools)
- a positive trauma recovery process (long-term therapy tools)

This book discusses each of these topics in roughly the order they are presented above. Before beginning, I am assuming you have at least a rudimentary grasp on the major writing craft techniques. If you do not know what an adverb or cliché are, let alone why you should actively avoid them like the plague (and why you can, sometimes, get away with them), there are many wonderful writing craft books, workshops, and courses available for you to gain this essential knowledge. Refer to the *Recommended Reading and References* section at the back of this book for several recommendations.

Although it will prove an advantage if you have a vague idea of the trauma elements you want to write — because you will be able to complete the suggested questions and exercises immediately — it is not necessary. This book can guide you through developing the idea if you complete the suggested questions and exercises at the end of the upcoming chapters. If you belong to this 'no idea' group, make sure you note down any ideas as they come so you can come back and finish (or update) the questions and exercises once a more solid idea forms.

I also want to signal here that I approach the topic of trauma from a Western perspective. As such, the information in this book *may not* apply to all cultural backgrounds, all historical time frames, and all intergenerational trauma situations. If you plan to incorporate aspects of trauma outside of this scope, you might need to research further for a deeper understanding.

Moreover, to avoid accidental misgendering and sexist language, I use the gender-neutral terms they/their when quoting other people in this book. I refer to myself by my pronouns she/her.

How is This Book Different?

During my PhD research, I discovered that little research had been undertaken in the academic space on the authentic representation of trauma in fiction. I also found limited non-fiction writing books providing well-informed advice on the subject. Being a trauma subgenre writer and academic, this posed a serious problem which prompted me to pen this book. As such, not only is this book filling a much-needed information gap for writers, but it is also fully backed by current research.

It does not matter whether you are yet to write your first draft or have written those exciting words 'The End' since *The Trauma-Informed Writer* will lead you through a series of questions and exercises which can enable you to finish an outline or assist you in refining the trauma elements of your complete manuscript. You can use a fresh notebook or computer-based document to complete the questions and exercises.

Why am I Qualified to Write This Book?

I have a Masters in Writing and a PhD in Creative Arts (writing), and am a multi-published fiction and non-fiction author of over 20 books. The books have been published by Pan Macmillan, Harlequin, and Serenade Publishing. My PhD thesis — which was awarded the title of 'one of the top 10% of outstanding theses in the field' — focused on the post-trauma romance subgenre – which combines specific aspects of trauma fiction and romance fiction.

During my PhD research, I also discovered several innovative trauma theories (including the Fade trauma response), which led to my international recognition as an emerging trauma theorist. Furthermore, I hold a Postgraduate Certificate in Counselling Skills, a Postgraduate Certificate in Psychology, and am currently completing a Graduate Diploma in Psychology. I am also a complex trauma survivor. Thus, I possess personal, industry, and educational knowledge in the fields of trauma and creative writing.

How is This Book Arranged?

I have arranged this book so you can gain an overview of the information necessary to write trauma elements. Each chapter expands upon the previous one by adding more information. The chapters were designed to make the sometimes-dense material more manageable, so please do not skip chapters. If you are short on time, you can choose to flick straight to the questions and exercises sections included at the end of each chapter. Though you will miss some of the more nuanced information, you can still gain a basic understanding of the essential concepts by doing this. Examples of the different trauma elements in popular fiction are also offered throughout this book to aid in your understanding of the concepts.

With the preliminaries over, let us start you on your path to becoming a trauma-informed writer!

Chapter 2 – Your Trigger Limiting Plan

A trigger limiting plan is a plan designed to reduce any possible triggers — anything which can cause a post-trauma response — throughout your writing process. Why is this important? The two short personal stories that follow provide the answer.

My debut novel, *See Her Run*, centred around a woman named Diana King who is on the run from her abusive ex-husband. Throughout the novel, Diana embarks on a *conscious* trauma recovery journey which involves facing the effects of the multiple traumas she survived in the marriage. I will circle back to the significance of your characters making a conscious choice later in this book. For now, I want to share an important lesson I learned while writing *See Her Run*. As you can likely glean from the brief synopsis, the story includes several trauma elements. When the initial idea came to me, I dove straight into the writing without stopping to think about the possibility, as a complex trauma survivor, of retraumatisation or experiencing vicarious/secondary trauma effects.

What is retraumatisation? I define retraumatisation as a trauma survivor being exposed to situations which force them to relive their traumatic experiences. Since I was writing elements which forced me to relive parts of my traumatic history — remember, many first novels are semi-autobiographical — I had inadvertently exposed myself to retraumatisation. Indeed, it caused massive upheavals in my personal life (including a minor psychological and existential breakdown). Contrast this episode in my life with the writing experience throughout my PhD, which focused on representing trauma in romance fiction. Due to the unforeseen consequences of writing *See Her Run*, I now understood the possibility of retraumatisation and prepared myself beforehand: I became trauma-informed. I started seeing an unorthodox trauma therapy psychologist (due to my lack of progress with an orthodox practitioner as well as my increased interest in the unorthodox) months before sitting down to write. I also made the choice to inform both my host university — Central Queensland University in the state of Queensland, Australia — and my amazing supervisory team about my trauma history. The slower pace of writing necessitated through the PhD journey helped to a certain extent and might also assist you. My thesis also required a tremendous amount of trauma theory research, understanding, and application, both personally and during the process of writing *The Love Healer* (the post-trauma romance novel I wrote for the creative part of my PhD thesis). This strong foundation resulted in milder, more manageable retraumatisation effects once I started writing. The other difference I noticed was a higher ratio of positive psychological effects.

Even though these are both anecdotal experiences — and should not be taken alone as incontrovertible 'proof' that being trauma-informed prevents retraumatisation for writers with a trauma background — the opinions of many other experts align with my experiences. For instance, renowned literary critic Shoshana Felman and psychoanalyst Dori Laub say talking about trauma can be dangerous because the 'price of speaking is re-living'. I argued in my PhD thesis that, equally, the price of *reading* and *writing* about trauma is a form of reliving, which can cause (or 'trigger') retraumatisation. Therefore, if you are a trauma survivor, I urge you to take care when it comes to writing (and reading) about trauma, especially if it is your first time tackling trauma in your fiction. One way you can do this is by creating what I call your 'trigger limiting plan'.

Your Trigger Limiting Plan – Part 1

I strongly advise authors with a trauma history attempting to write a trauma-themed story, to create a 'trigger limiting plan' before writing. In this plan, include details about how you will:

- organise a solid support system (family, friends, counsellors, etc.)
- slow down the writing process to give your brain, body, and nervous system (referred to throughout this book as the 'BBANS') time to adjust to the trauma elements without overloading your ability to cope. You might also choose to break up the days you write the trauma scenes.
- provide self-care on the days you write trauma scenes
- set up regular check-in appointments with yourself and/or a member of your support system to manage any early warning signs of retraumatisation
- manage any retraumatisation effects which appear

• note anything else you think might help.

What about vicarious/secondary/second-hand trauma? These terms refer to the appearance of post-trauma effects after witnessing, but not personally experiencing, a trauma (such as seeing someone being robbed at gunpoint), listening to someone recount their traumatic experiences (like many mental health care nurses are expected to do), and even reading about traumatic events (like the holocaust and natural disasters). Since writing your novel will involve trauma-related research, which includes reading this book, you may unwittingly expose yourself to trauma narratives which can impact you in the form of vicarious/secondary/second-hand trauma. As per retraumatisation, there are several ways to limit the impact on you and your mental health. One way is to complete part 2 of your trigger limiting plan detailed below.

Your Trigger Limiting Plan – Part 2

Many of the points you made in part 1 of this plan will overlap here. However, I want you to think specifically about the trauma-related research you will need to undertake. Do you have personal experience of the trauma you are writing about? If not, how can you boost your knowledge of the trauma so you can write about it in a sensitive way? Is there an historical event you need to understand more deeply before you can write about it with historical accuracy (example: 9/11)? Will you need to interview witnesses/survivors of a certain trauma to add authenticity? What books might you have to read which contain traumatic details? Are there any documentaries or podcasts which can supplement your knowledge (avoid movies since they notoriously misrepresent trauma)? The answers to these questions offer insight into potential triggers. Write these possible triggers into your plan, then:
• ensure you space out the days and times you plan to read/interview/watch/listen (write specific dates in your plan if you need to)
• inform your support network of the potential need for extra support and attention on research days
• engage in extra self-care
• stop if you experience anything which makes you feel distressed and seek

immediate assistance. In your plan, write down who you will call, how you will seek help, and any pertinent numbers, addresses, and websites.

Since you are writing fiction, you are, technically, absolved from the broader consequences of your writing as it applies to your readers. Even so, part of the responsibility of being a trauma-informed writer, in my opinion, is considering the potential effects on your readers as well. Retraumatisation and vicarious/secondary/second-hand trauma can impact your readers in several ways, some of which you might not have ever thought about. As a trauma-informed writer, it is time to start thinking about it.

Firstly, ask yourself whether your trauma representations could trigger trauma-based reactions in your readers, not only from reading about the trauma itself, but also due to inaccurate, insensitive, and inauthentic representations. For instance, older novels which 'victim blame' female survivors of sexual assault by writing the story in a way which puts the cause of the assault on the shoulders of the survivor — for instance, by stating that she was wearing a short skirt, walked home alone in the dark, or flirted — are severely problematic and retraumatising. Do you 'victim blame' in your manuscript? Is there a plot-driven purpose for it? Is it resolved? If not, why have you written it like this?

Secondly, ponder the way you have/plan to represent the trauma elements. Do they align with the research you have (or will have) carried out? Have you consistently followed the guidelines in this book? Do you know enough about trauma to write it with sensitivity, authenticity, and accuracy? If not, how can you achieve this?

Thirdly, let's discuss trigger warnings. The research which has been carried out on trigger warnings shows mixed results. This means they could help ... or they might make the situation worse. Reactions to reading a trigger warning seem to come down to the traumatised individual, so there is no blanket rule when it comes to trigger warnings. Personally, it depends how I feel in the moment as to whether I include a trigger warning or not. You can feel free to do the same since, due to the current research, the benefits of including a trigger warning are still up for debate. Alternatively, you could think about adding a simple 'note to readers' warning them of potential disturbing content. You might have noticed that I did not include an overt trigger warning for this book on the front cover. I made that choice because I felt the title of the book would prime readers as to the contents!

Finally, it is time to complete part 3 of your trigger limiting plan by adding aspects to limit trauma triggers for your readers.

Your Trigger Limiting Plan – Part 3

Add the following points to your trigger limiting plan:

- removal of victim blaming (if victim blaming forms an important plot point in your book, ensure it is explicitly over-ruled by the end of the manuscript)
- a final checklist. This checklist will include ensuring you have represented the traumatic event or experience, trauma responses, post-trauma effects, and trauma recovery in a way that is sensitive, authentic, and accurate
- trigger warning? Ponder whether it is worthwhile to include a trigger warning. If you decide to include one, how would you do it? Will you use a simple note on the front cover or blurb, saying, 'This book contains trauma elements' or something more complex, such as, 'This book contains depictions of *list of specifics*'?
- resource list. Will you include a list of helpful resources at the end of the book to aid anyone triggered or to offer further information?
- anything else you can think of.

You have now completed your trigger limiting plan. The subsequent chapters contain various levels of trauma information. I stress that, should you proceed in reading this book, completing the suggested questions and exercises, formulating an outline for your novel, or using this book to refine the trauma elements in your final draft, you may experience challenging, upsetting, or triggering moments. Please proceed with caution, a sturdy support network, and a complete trigger limiting plan. If you are not reading this book for information around crafting trauma into a book manuscript, please feel free to skip forward to chapter 5 (understanding trauma).

Chapter 3 – Your Main Fiction Genre Plus the Trauma Genre Equals Your Trauma-Themed Subgenre

Although you can successfully infuse <u>any</u> genre with trauma elements, certain genres are more apt to portray trauma based on their inherent features, for instance:

- trauma genre
- romance genre
- crime genre

This does not mean you have to write in one of these genres if you want to add trauma elements into your story, only that it <u>may</u> be harder when writing in another genre. Something else to consider is:

You Will be Writing a Trauma-Themed Subgenre

Based on my PhD research, the trauma genre is 'a work of fiction which incorporates an element of trauma representation into its storyline'. Besides straight trauma fiction, any other main fiction genre you choose to incorporate trauma representation into will also slot your work into the trauma genre. How can you write in two genres? Basically, you cannot. But you *can* write in a trauma-themed subgenre.

Subgenres have their own unique features and conventions. Yes, this can get confusing, which is why you need to have a solid understanding of your main genre's conventions and expectations before applying trauma elements to it. This book can help you to weave the trauma elements into your main genre to help you form a corresponding trauma-themed subgenre. However, you will need to research the precise conventions which apply to your subgenre. If I included a list of all the relevant conventions and expectations of the multitude of trauma-themed subgenres open to you, this book would blow out to an untenable size. Even so, I can provide some guidance towards discerning your subgenre (so you can research it) and what trauma elements to include.

Subgenres and Trauma Elements

The publishing industry is full of writers obsessed with knowing where their book fits into the scheme of things. So are academics — I had to write an entire section of my PhD on the nuances of genre and subgenre. Full disclosure: I am only qualified and experienced enough to comment with full confidence on the trauma-themed romance subgenres. But I can take an educated guess, and give you a simple formula, along with relevant book examples, to assist you in deducing your specific brand of trauma-themed subgenre. By zeroing in on your subgenre, you will understand which trauma elements to mix into your main genre features. Let's start with the three major trauma-themed romance subgenres, namely, trauma romance, post-trauma romance, and transitional post-trauma romance.

1. Trauma Romance (TR) is 'a work of fiction that depicts a traumatic experience/s within a romantic narrative'. It has the following features:
   - a central love story
   - a HEA (happily-ever-after) or HFN (happy-for-now) ending
   - at least one traumatised main character
   - a depiction of the trauma
   - may feature minor depictions of trauma responses and post-trauma effects

Trauma Romance examples include *Guild Boss* by Jayne Ann Krentz (writing as Jayne Castle) and *The Duke and I* by Julia Quinn. Table 1 contains a breakdown of each trauma element appearing in the books (warning: spoilers for both books appear in the table).

Trauma Element	*Guild Boss* by Jayne Castle (2021)	*The Duke and I* by Julia Quinn (2000)
Central love story with a HEA or HFN	Has a central love story with a HEA ending between a heroine (Lucy) and hero (Gabriel).	Has a central love story with a HEA ending between a heroine (Daphne) and hero (Simon).

Traumatised character	Heroine is shown to have experienced trauma.	Hero is shown to have experienced trauma.
Trauma described/ explored/ depicted	Heroine was kidnapped and drugged (but nobody believes her).	Hero endured abuse by his father.
Minor depictions of trauma responses and/ or post-trauma effects	Not evident.	Hero displays minor trauma responses (shaking in his father's presence as a flood response) and minor post-trauma effects (hypervigilance when he speaks). Note: since it can be argued that Simon not wanting children impacts his marriage, *The Duke and I* can also slot into the Transitional Post-Trauma Romance (TPTR)

Table 1: Trauma Romance Examples
Source: Author

2. Post-Trauma Romance (PTR) is 'a work of fiction that depicts a traumatic experience/s, its post-trauma effects, and the processes of recovery from the traumatic experience/s within a romantic narrative'. It has the following features:

- a central love story
- a HEA or HFN ending
- at least one traumatised main character
- a depiction of the trauma
- a depiction of trauma responses and post-trauma effects, whether minor or major
- showing how the post-trauma effects impact the developing romantic relationship/s
- a depiction of conscious and positive trauma recovery attempts

Post-Trauma Romance examples include my novels, writing as A.K. Leigh, *See Her Run* and *The Love Healer*. Table 2 contains a breakdown of each feature as it appears in the books (spoilers for both books also appear in this table).

Trauma Element	*See Her Run* by A.K. Leigh (2015)	*The Love Healer* by A.K. Leigh (2024)
Central love story with a HEA or HFN	Has a central love story with a HEA ending between a heroine (Diana) and hero (Jonathan).	Has a central love story with a HFN ending between a heroine (Neoma) and hero (Emerson).
Traumatised character	Both heroine and hero are shown to have experienced trauma.	Both heroine and hero are shown to have experienced trauma.
Trauma described/ explored/depicted	Heroine's trauma is from abuse in her marriage. The hero's is through an abusive father.	Heroine's trauma is from an assault and sexual harassment. The hero's is via his time as a military psychologist.
Trauma responses and post-trauma effects described and/or explored	Diana is shown to experience the Flight, Fawn, Fade, and Faint trauma responses with PTSD among her post-trauma effects. Jonathan is portrayed with several post-trauma defence mechanisms.	Neoma is shown to experience the Flood, Freeze, Fright, and Fade trauma responses with CPTSD and defence mechanisms among her post-trauma effects. Emerson is shown to experience the Flood, Flight, and Fade trauma responses with PTSD and coping mechanisms among his post-trauma effects.

Post-trauma effects shown to impact the relationship	Diana's PTSD slows down the developing relationship. Jonathan's defence mechanisms cause their initial breakup.	Neoma employs multiple defence mechanisms, which slows their connection. Emerson's coping and defence mechanisms also interfere with the relationship.
Conscious and *positive* trauma recovery attempts represented	Diana attends conventional talk therapy throughout.	Neoma attends unorthodox therapy. Emerson sees a therapist towards the end.

Table 2: Post-Trauma Romance Examples
Source: Author

3. Transitional Post-Trauma Romance (TPTR) is a work of fiction which straddles the line between trauma romance and post-trauma romance by depicting a traumatic experience/s and some post-trauma features within a romantic narrative. It has the following features:
   - a central love story
   - a HEA or HFN ending
   - at least one traumatised main character
   - a depiction of the trauma
   - Plus one or two of the following three features (note: only 1 or 2 of the features listed below can appear in a TPTR, otherwise it is a PTR!):
   - a depiction of minor trauma responses and/or post-trauma effects
   - showing how the post-trauma effects impact the developing romantic relationship/s
   - a minor depiction of conscious and positive trauma recovery attempts

Transitional Post-Trauma Romance examples include *It Ends With Us* by Colleen Hoover and *The Tenant of Wildfell Hall* by Emily Brontë. Table 3 contains a breakdown of each feature as it appears in the books (naturally, spoilers for both books occur in the table).

Trauma Element	*It Ends With Us* by Colleen Hoover (2016)	*The Tenant of Wildfell Hall* by Anne Brontë (1848)
Central love story with a HEA or HFN	Has a central love story with a HFN ending between a heroine (Lily) and hero (Atlas).	Has a central love story with a HEA ending between a heroine (Helen) and hero (Gilbert).
Traumatised character	Both heroine and hero are shown to have experienced trauma.	Heroine is shown to have experienced trauma.
Trauma described/explored/depicted	Heroine's trauma is depicted as vicarious (witnessing her father's abuse of her mother) and abuse in her marriage. The hero's is through an abusive stepfather and abandoning mother.	Helen has survived an abusive marriage with an alcoholic, cheating, gambling husband.
Trauma responses and post-trauma effects described and/or explored	Heroine shows some Fawn trauma responses (when she placates her husband during his abuse) and minor post-trauma effects.	Heroine is depicted with minor Fade and Fight trauma responses and minor post-trauma effects (defence mechanisms around not trusting men and being wary of alcohol drinkers).
Post-trauma effects shown to impact the relationship	Lily wants time to get through her pregnancy and divorce before addressing the relationship. This can be argued to be a post-trauma effects defence mechanism.	Helen refuses to marry Gilbert until some time has passed and she can trust herself not to naively rush into another marriage too soon. Like *It Ends With Us*, this can be seen as a defence mechanism.

Conscious and *positive* trauma recovery attempts represented	Not evident.	Significantly, considering the time it was written, Helen indulges in painting. The activity is shown to bring her both money and peace. This can be viewed as a form of 'art therapy' by modern standards. Even so, since it was not depicted as a conscious recovery attempt (likely because Western conceptions of trauma recovery were in their infancy at the time) *Tenant* cannot count as PTR.

Table 3: Transitional Post-Trauma Romance Examples
Source: Author

As you have, hopefully, been able to discern from the provided definitions, features, and book examples, each trauma-themed romance subgenre can be differentiated from the others through comparison. Theoretically, the same applies to your own trauma-themed subgenre. In other words, it can be differentiated according to its features. By using the names and features of the trauma-themed romance subgenres as a guide, the specific name and features of your trauma-themed subgenre can be extrapolated. I have included two simple guides to assist you in working these out for yourself.

What Trauma Elements to Include

To refresh your memory, there are several trauma elements you can include in your novel. These are:

- trauma representation (including vicarious/secondary trauma, so long as it is represented)
- initial trauma response
- post-trauma effects
- post-trauma recovery
- impact on the romantic relationship

If you have not decided on the trauma elements you would like to include in your story, now is the time. Here are the basic guidelines to consider:

1. For trauma-only subgenres, you need to include:

- trauma representation

2. For post-trauma subgenres, you need to include:

- trauma representation
- initial trauma response/post-trauma effects
- post-trauma recovery
- impact on romantic relationship

3. For transitional post-trauma subgenres, you need to include:

- trauma representation

AND <u>one or two of:</u>

- initial trauma response/post-trauma effects
- post-trauma recovery
- impact on romantic relationship

Zeroing in on the trauma elements you want to include now will make it easier when it comes to plotting and representing the trauma when you write. But having the trauma elements decided, does not necessarily mean you know the name of your subgenre. That is where the next section can assist you.

Defining the Name of Your Trauma-Themed Subgenre

Below is a (simplified and imperfect) three-step formula I have created to help you work out your trauma-themed subgenre's name.

Step 1: Take your main fiction genre (example: crime)

Step 2: Add the word 'trauma' before the main genre (example: trauma crime*)

Step 3: Apply your trauma elements

- do you want to focus mainly on a representation of the trauma? (Stop at step 2)
- do you want to include trauma responses and post-trauma effects, an impact on the romantic relationship/s, and trauma recovery? (Add the word 'post-' before 'trauma'. Example: post-trauma crime)

27

- do you want to incorporate some of the above trauma elements but not all of them? (Add the words 'transitional post-' before trauma. Example: transitional post-trauma crime)

*I categorise Stephen King's recent novel, *Holly*, as a trauma crime novel. This is because it depicts the main character, private investigator Holly Gibney, experiencing a trauma/s ('trauma') while investigating disappearances ('crime').

Here are some other possible trauma-themed subgenres to inspire your imagination:

- Trauma Fantasy, Post-Trauma Fantasy, Transitional Post-Trauma Fantasy
- Trauma Horror, Post-Trauma Horror, Transitional Post-Trauma Horror
- Trauma Dystopian, Post-Trauma Dystopian, Transitional Post-Trauma Dystopian
- Trauma Mystery, Post-Trauma Mystery, Transitional Post-Trauma Mystery
- Trauma Thriller, Post-Trauma Thriller, Transitional Post-Trauma Thriller
- Trauma Sci-Fi, Post-Trauma Sci-Fi, Transitional Post-Trauma Sci-Fi
- Trauma Adventure, Post-Trauma Adventure, Transitional Post-Trauma Adventure
- Trauma Romantasy, Post-Trauma Romantasy, Transitional Post-Trauma Romantasy
- Trauma Paranormal, Post-Trauma Paranormal, Transitional Post-Trauma Paranormal
- Trauma Historical, Post-Trauma Historical, Transitional Post-Trauma Historical (naturally, you would also need to consider the relevant historical context around trauma)
- Trauma Literary, Post-Trauma Literary, Transitional Post-Trauma Literary
- Trauma Magic Realism, Post-Trauma Magic Realism, Transitional Post-Trauma Magic Realism
- Trauma Spec-fic, Post-Trauma Spec-fic, Transitional Post-Trauma Spec-fic

In case you are a more visual thinker, Table 4 highlights the connection between the trauma-themed subgenre name and its associated trauma elements to guide you further.

Trauma-Themed Subgenre Name	Trauma Elements
'Trauma main genre' Example: trauma crime	• Your main fiction genre's features • At least one traumatised main character • Trauma representation
'Post-trauma main genre' Example: post-trauma fantasy	• Your main fiction genre's features • At least one traumatised main character • Representation of the trauma • Depiction of the post-trauma effects • Depiction of the trauma recovery journey
'Transitional post-trauma main genre' Example: transitional post-trauma horror	• Your main fiction genre's features • At least one traumatised main character • Representation of the trauma • One or two of: depictions of trauma responses and post-trauma effects, post-trauma effects shown to impact a romantic relationship • A conscious *and* positive trauma recovery journey attempt

Table 4: Trauma-Themed Subgenre Naming Conventions and Their Associated Trauma Elements
Source: Author

Another important point to note at this stage: the passing mention of a past or present trauma in the story cannot be classified as including trauma elements. This is because it does not fulfil the inherent 'representation' requirement of a trauma-themed subgenre. I refer to the brief mention of trauma in a story somewhat interchangeably as 'background trauma' and 'non-trauma' fiction. Think of it this way: if you mention a character is the survivor of a crime in their past, does that mean you have written a crime novel? Of course not, there are particular conventions you need to have met to fit your story into that genre. The same applies to the trauma-themed subgenres. You will want to avoid purely background trauma when writing trauma-themed subgenres.

It is also fine if your understanding of trauma is limited — or based on popular conception — at this stage. That is what this book is for; it will introduce you step-by-step to each of the related concepts and theory, deepen previous understanding, and expand upon the ideas of previous chapters. Right now, all you need is to have a clear idea of the subgenre name and its associated features.

Questions and Exercises

*You might want to refer to Tables 1–4 to complete these questions and exercises.

1. What is the name of your trauma-themed subgenre?

2. What features will you need to incorporate into your story? (Consider both the trauma elements as well as the main genre characteristics)

3. If your proposed trauma is 'background only', have a think about ways you can bring that background trauma to the foreground. Subsequent chapters may help you achieve that. Even so, it can prove helpful at this point to make notes: you might be surprised by what you instinctively know.

4. If you have a trauma plot which you feel is not background only, write down the general overview of it (include which characters are involved, what the traumatic event/experience is, etc.).

5. How will you represent/depict/explore the trauma in your manuscript?

Chapter 4 – Overview of the Major Arcs

Before completing your novel, you will also need to incorporate three major Arcs into the plot: the character arc, trauma arc, and (possibly) relationship arc. Since you should have a foundational knowledge of arcs, the following provides an overview of each arc only.

What is the Character Arc?

As stated in my non-fiction book, *The Romance Novel Formula*, the character arc 'refers to the way the characters grow, change, and mature as the story unfolds'. Clearly, the trauma story is going to impact the character and, therefore, this arc. You will need to map out the ways your character will change throughout the story due to their personal trauma journey. The information and questions/exercises provided throughout this book are designed to help with parts of that process. However, think about this arc now — where will your character start and where will they end up?

What is the Trauma Arc?

The trauma arc narrows in on and tracks the trauma elements of the story. These trauma elements include the traumatic experience, any initial trauma responses, post-trauma effects, and post-trauma recovery attempts. Again, the following chapters will assist in outlining this arc, but thinking about it now will help.

What is the Relationship Arc?

You may plan to represent post-trauma effects in your storyline. If you do, and the plot includes interactions between a traumatised individual and other characters, you might want to think about the impact of trauma on these relationships, especially romantic ones. You will need to align the relationship arc to your main genre expectations as well as your chosen trauma-themed subgenre features. Some of these will not require you to think about relationship impact (such as the trauma-only subgenres), whereas others might (post-trauma, definitely; transitional post-trauma, maybe). Revisit the previous chapter for a refresher on the requirements for each subgenre should you need it.

Questions and Exercises

1. Jot down any ideas you have for how your character will grow, change, and mature as the story unfolds (character arc). You should gain a better understanding of this arc as you read this book, but it is still good practice to note down your initial ideas now.

2. The same applies to the trauma arc. Although you will have a deeper knowledge of trauma and the trauma recovery journey by the end of this book, jotting down any intuitive insights now can help later when you have more knowledge to apply.

3. How do you think trauma might impact on the romantic relationships in your story?

4. How do you think trauma might impact on the non-romantic relationships in your story?

Chapter 5 – Understanding Trauma

It would be wonderful if I could unequivocally state, 'trauma is such and such'. However, I cannot do that because the question around what constitutes trauma is highly contested within academic circles. Why is that? To begin with, the term 'trauma' originally *only* denoted a physical wound as opposed to the mental/psychological/emotional wound the term has come to mean in contemporary times. Furthermore, as Sadiya Abubakar notes, the words 'trauma theory' were used for the first time by Cathy Caruth in their book *Unclaimed Experience* in 1996. Yes, you read that right: **1996**. Hence, the theory around trauma is relatively new ... despite the common misconception that trauma theory started with Sigmund Freud in the late 1800s.

Even with these challenges, I was able to find a workable definition, accepted by most academics, during my PhD research. Before I offer that definition, fix the following idea firmly in your mind: trauma is <u>not</u> a minor, inconvenient, or flippant experience. As such, it should not be used in an off-hand way in your writing (or everyday life). Trauma is a serious experience with equally serious consequences for individuals (and generations, cultures, marginalised groups, and nations).

With that proviso given, my definition of trauma is 'an experience/s which threatens feelings of safety and subsequent ideas of the self'. Let me unpack this definition:

Firstly, trauma is an *experience* (i.e., something that happens). This experience can be physical (e.g., a bank robbery), emotional (e.g., constant belittling and invalidation), mental/psychological (e.g., severe gaslighting), visual (e.g., witnessing an horrific accident), verbal (e.g., repetitive name-calling), sexual (e.g., childhood molestation or sexual harassment), financial (e.g., being scammed out of one's life savings), and a host of many other experiences. Of course, it can also be — and usually is — a combination of any or all of these.

Secondly, this experience *threatens feelings of safety* (i.e., it causes fear and/or makes someone feel like they will be harmed). This threat to feelings of safety can, again, come in a myriad of ways: psychologically, emotionally, physically, sexually, and so forth.

Thirdly, the experience also *threatens ideas of the self* (i.e., it causes someone to question their identity). In other words, the experience has to have been serious enough, and threatening enough, to also cause an individual to question their identity. What do I mean by 'identity'? I mean someone's sense of themselves — what they see as their core characteristics, beliefs, values, roles, and the aspects that make them unique to others. It also relates to how they see themselves in the world, how they view others, and how they believe others view them. Often accompanied by questions, such as: who am I? What is life for? Why did I survive? Why me? What did I do wrong? Did I do something to deserve this?

If these three parts are not present, a particular incident cannot (usually) be classed as a trauma or traumatic. Need an example of this in action? Let me introduce you to Sieg, he will be our example trauma survivor character throughout. Sieg is a bank manager who was singled out in a bank robbery (at his bank, when he was on duty) and had a knife held to his throat. He has struggled with going to work (due to the memories) and 'finding his feet' since the bank robbery. Using the above trauma definition as a base, we can see that:

a) Sieg had something happen to him (the bank robbery in which he was singled out)

b) it threatened his feelings of safety (having a knife to his throat made him feel like he could be harmed)

c) it altered his view of himself and his place in the world (e.g., 'the bank is no longer a safe place for me to work' and 'who am I if I am not a bank manager?')

These three parts are what you will need to make sure you have nailed in your own manuscript. Do not worry if you do not have these details worked out yet, that is what the questions and exercises section is for.

Another important consideration before we move on: my trauma definition encompasses by-proxy exposure to a threatening event as well as personal exposure, namely, it incorporates primary as well as vicarious/secondary/second-hand trauma. The definition also has the important inclusion of the words 'ideas of the self'. This reflects how trauma causes a shift in how a person views themselves and their place in the world; it alters their identity ... sometimes drastically. For example, a trauma survivor can move from seeing themselves as

34

confident pre-trauma to unsure of themselves post-trauma. The shift can also include their identity being 'safe in the world' before the trauma, but now they have a sense that 'they are forever unsafe'. Under this definition, then, an everyday, inconvenient event diverges from trauma, since a minor annoyance is unlikely to affect how someone views themselves, but a traumatic event will. See how, if even one of the three definition elements is not there, it can change the story as well as the potential impact of the trauma on the character?

Now, think about whether your proposed trauma fits the provided definition of trauma: *an experience/s which threatens feelings of safety and subsequent ideas of the self.* Will the trauma be enough to affect your character to the point that it changes their ideas of themselves/their identity? Does it affect the level of safety they feel, both during and after the event? Before writing any of the other trauma elements, you need to have a solid idea of the traumatic experience that your character/s will encounter. The proffered trauma definition starts with an *experience.* What happened to your character? Was it physical, emotional, mental/psychological, visual, verbal, sexual, financial, or a combination?

One you have the experience decided, you will need to work on ways to represent it with authenticity, accuracy, and sensitivity in your work. How do you do that? Depending on the chosen experience, the answer to this will differ — remember, there are no definites in trauma theory! Unfortunately, I cannot include a complete 'show X if you want to include Y trauma'. There are simply too many potential traumas to have representation notes for all of them in an introductory level book. As such, you will need to carry out a certain level of research into your chosen traumatic event, unless you are writing from personal experience. If you are reading this book with an intention other than to write trauma-themed fiction, you might think gathering these details is not applicable to you. However, **all** trauma-informed writers should know the facts of any trauma they are writing about. Therefore, some specific topics you might want to research include:

- <u>what</u> is the traumatic event (so this is clear in your mind before researching)?
- <u>how</u> does the traumatic experience most commonly occur (by accident, with a gun, fire)?
- <u>how long</u> does the traumatic experience most commonly last (minutes, hours, weeks, months, years)?

35

- <u>when</u> does the traumatic experience most commonly occur (childhood, noon, during family holidays)?
- <u>where</u> does the traumatic experience most commonly occur (at home, in the street, at school)?
- <u>what</u> are the most common elements of the traumatic experience (is there a pattern)?
- if a crime is involved, <u>who</u> is the most common perpetrator?
- <u>who</u> is the most common victim/survivor?

Once you have carried out this research, ponder whether your chosen traumatic experience align with the research? By understanding what the research says about these aspects of your chosen traumatic event, you are more likely to write it in an authentic (and accurate) way. For instance, let us return to Sieg and the bank robbery. Possible answers to the above questions could be the following (please note: I have *not* researched this beyond a cursory look, I am simply providing an example to show you how you might answer these questions):

- <u>what</u> is the traumatic event?
  - Sieg is held up at knife point during a bank robbery.
- <u>how</u> does the traumatic experience most commonly occur?
  - With intimidation tactics by a group of people and/or the use of knives (Australia has gun laws, making bank robberies via guns less likely).
- <u>how long</u> does the traumatic experience most commonly last (minutes, hours, weeks, months, years)?
  - Minutes, to avoid apprehension by police.
- <u>when</u> does the traumatic experience most commonly occur (childhood, noon, during family holidays)?
  - When the bank is less busy to allow for quick entry and exit by the robbers.
- <u>where</u> does the traumatic experience most commonly occur (at home, in the street, at school)?
  - at a bank.
- <u>what</u> are the most common elements of the traumatic experience (is there a pattern)?
  - Customers are told to lie face-down on the floor, security personnel are disarmed, a 'lookout' stands out the front of the bank, there is a 'getaway

car', one person takes charge, robbers have their faces covered, certain staff are singled out to access the money.

- if a crime is involved, <u>who</u> is the most common perpetrator?
  - White/European adult male (taken from the Australian Institute of Criminology data. It is the one piece of information I did research for this task!).
- <u>who</u> is the most common victim/survivor?
  - Bank staff and customers.

Once you have used your research skills to uncover the answers to the above questions, you now have the 'facts' of the traumatic experience. These facts can be used to write your authentic (and accurate) event. In the case of Sieg, the above facts align with the basic story idea presented, so I could continue with this traumatic event with a high-level of accuracy.

What about you? At this point, you may have realised you need other information not covered by the above list of questions. This is common in research, so do not panic. If you need to carry out another phase of research, go ahead and do that now, then come back and finish reading this chapter.

When you are happy with the information gathered in your research stage, think about whether you want to change any of the plot points to reflect your research or whether it is fine to keep the plot as it is. Returning to Sieg, if I had decided upon a white female as the main bank robber, this still corresponds to the research, so I could keep it in the story; a small percentage of white women <u>do</u> commit bank robberies (again, this is based on the Australian data). But I, like you, can only know this after carrying out the research. This simple example shows you one reason why it is important to get the facts about your traumatic event before attempting to write about it.

As a trauma-informed writer, you will also want to consider ways to write about these events with a high level of sensitivity and compassion. Many trauma survivors possess a strong and misguided sense of shame or guilt post-trauma. Hence, in keeping with the ethical considerations for your readers — who may have encountered the traumatic event you are planning to portray — you will want to ensure you write about it with a measured level of sensitivity. To achieve this:

- remove 'victim blaming' and victim blaming language (unless it is part of the plot that will be resolved in a positive way by the end of your manuscript, but even then, *tread carefully*)
- have a sensitivity reader (or qualified editor) look over your trauma event scenes
- focus on representing the 'facts', as uncovered during your research
- focus on the story sequence – this happened, then that happened, then this happened
- remove judgements from the narrator
- learn as much as you can about trauma, the way people respond to it, and its common lingering effects (like this book explores)
- go over your trigger limiting plan. Are you sticking to it as closely as possible?

Something else you may want to consider in your writing is trauma 'type' — though this is an optional inclusion because the concept of trauma type is debated (along with everything else in trauma theory). Some theorists claim that traumatic experiences can be categorised as:

- acute (from a once-off event)
- chronic (from a prolonged or multiple experience)

To clarify, a prolonged experience is one that continues for an extended amount of time, such as torture or domestic violence, and a multiple experience is an accumulation of acute/once-off events. In the case of Sieg, the bank robbery would be considered a 'once off/acute' trauma type event. However, if Sieg has experienced other traumas, then the bank robbery can push him over into the 'multiple/chronic' trauma type. Trauma types are explored in more detail in upcoming chapters but are mentioned now to lay the basis for this later discussion. Have a think about whether your chosen trauma would correspond to an acute or chronic experience. Ask yourself whether it is a once-off traumatic event or a prolonged traumatic event. If you want to remain accurate, authentic, and sensitive in your trauma writing, the decisions you make about the proposed traumatic experience and its associated type *can* (but not absolutely) influence the post-trauma effects you represent.

Questions and Exercises

1. Is your proposed trauma big enough to affect your character's ideas of themselves? Write some notes on how you will make the trauma impact your character's ideas of themselves.

2. Is your proposed trauma big enough to affect your character's feeling of safety <u>during</u> the experience? Note how the proposed trauma will achieve this. Is your proposed trauma big enough to affect your character's feelings of safety <u>after</u> the experience? Scribble your thoughts into your notebook.

3. Go to the suggested research questions, do your research, and write the answers in your notebook.

4. Is there any part of the traumatic event representation that you want to change now that you have researched it?

5. Have you written the traumatic experience with a level of sensitivity?

6. What trauma type does your chosen trauma seem to align with: chronic (prolonged/multiple) or acute (once-off)?

Chapter 6 – How to Represent Trauma in Your Writing with Authenticity, Accuracy, and Sensitivity

Like trauma theory, the correct way to represent trauma in writing remains a contested space in academia. Some theorists, such as Cathy Caruth, even assert that 'the trauma experience will and should remain inaccessible to representation'. Naturally, since I am writing this book (and have written multiple trauma-themed romance novels), I am one of the theorists who disagrees with Caruth's assessment. Indeed, there are several generally accepted ways to represent trauma in your novels.

These techniques can be broadly classified under two umbrella terms: what I call the literary method, or the way you *write the book*, and the plotting method, or the way you *write the plot events* which affect the characters. An important reminder: *all trauma-themed subgenres require some form of plotting method representation*, but they <u>do not</u> need literary method representation. Therefore, the inclusion of the literary method is up to personal preference (unless you are writing a trauma literary novel. In that instance, include the literary methods). Also, due to the newly theorised nature of trauma-themed subgenres, the specific writing techniques to use in these subgenres is still up for debate (and research). But while writing *The Love Healer*, I adapted my usual creative writing process and practice to experiment with common literary and literary trauma writing techniques and several plotting methods. That said, what are some of the main literary method and plotting method techniques?

The Plotting Method

At a minimum, you need to show/represent/depict the traumatic event or experience in your writing. Remember: *the trauma genre and trauma subgenres require trauma representation*. Write about it. Include it in the narrative. Show it happening. You can do this in several ways (pick one or all of the following. You can develop your own methods too):

- *in media res*: start your story 'in the middle of things', as the trauma is happening. Using the bank robbery example: from your first sentence, you would showcase the bank robbery scene; perhaps it starts with a literal *bang* (the robber slamming their hands on the counter)?
- *flashbacks:* have the traumatised character recall the traumatic event in flashbacks. Maybe Sieg is going about his day, when he walks past a bank and the glistening flash of a steel knife blade enters his head?
- *a dream/nightmare*: the character can dream about the experience. The dream could be a play-by-play of the traumatic experience, and you could incorporate nightmarish or surrealist symbolism into it (make sure the <u>actual</u> events are understood by the end of the book though). These dreams could also come in fragments, in a nightly series, or some combination, until the full event is revealed to the reader. Perhaps Sieg has a black-and-white dream sequence with 1920s gangsters blasting Tommy guns at each other — representing how his black and white view of the world has been upended through weapons?
- *therapy*: the trauma survivor can tell their trauma story to a therapist. This is delved into in more detail in subsequent chapters on trauma recovery (with a full sample session starring Sieg). However, the basic idea is to reveal parts of the traumatic event in each therapy session.
- *conversation*: have the traumatised character tell someone about it, or have another character ask them about it. This differs to the therapy option since it pertains to someone other than a therapist. It could be a trusted friend, a new love interest, or a parent (amongst other choices). Perhaps a colleague who was in the bank with Sieg on the day of the robbery notices his struggles and suggests he see a counsellor through the bank's Employee Assistance Program.
- *gossip/rumours*: other people can refer to what happened (either correctly or incorrectly). You could have other characters talking about rumours they had heard about the incident. Is Sieg's new love interest informed about the bank robbery from someone else?

- *good old-fashioned eavesdropping*: have characters eavesdrop or overhear conversations about the trauma. You could choose the traumatised character and/or other characters for this. Maybe Sieg overhears the gossiping in the previous example?
- *via the media*: employ television, social media, and news reports in telling the trauma story. In the bank robbery example, you could employ television news reports in the telling of the event.

The following chapters include further suggestions around the plotting method and its application to the specific trauma elements. You will also be asked to think about these possibilities in the questions and exercises section at the end of this chapter.

The literary method

There is also a plethora of options available when it comes to the literary method for representing trauma. The basic idea is to use writing techniques which mimic the symptoms, behaviours, and thoughts/feelings of trauma survivorship. Technically, any writing technique which mimics the thoughts, feelings, symptoms, and behaviours associated with trauma can be employed. You can really let your imagination run wild with the literary method. Following is an overview of some of the most recommended techniques along with those I used in writing *The Love Healer* and several of my other novels. Whilst not an exhaustive list (since more research needs to be carried out), I have used all of them with success in representing trauma. Thus, they are a solid place to start when thinking about using literary techniques.

Interior Monologues

As suggested by literary trauma expert Laurie Vickroy, interior monologues occur when a character is mentally talking to themselves. Therefore, any thoughts a character has is an interior monologue. How does this relate to trauma? One common post-trauma effect is persistent, repetitive (another way to represent repetition), and negative interior monologues. Also note: interior monologues are typically identified by the use of italics in a manuscript.

Example: *What do I do?*

Repetition/Repetition Compulsion

Sigmund Freud wrote about the 'repetition compulsion' common amongst his clients. In modern trauma theory parlance, the repetition compulsion refers to a trauma survivor being repeatedly exposed to the same or similar traumatic situations. This happens either through the individual themselves engaging in situations most likely to lead to a repeat of the trauma or through being more prone to end up in those same situations due to post-trauma effects. The compulsion is <u>not</u> intentional or conscious, and survivors should <u>never</u> be blamed for experiencing this common, normal effect. It is well-established in the academic literature that someone who was abused as a child is more prone to being abused as an adult. In neither case is the individual at fault. This is the repetition compulsion in action. Various theories exist which explain this effect, including the subconscious mind's attempt at 'completing the trauma' in a way which halts unpleasant post-trauma effects. To portray the repetition compulsion in your work, you might want to use:

- repetitive character thoughts, feelings, and behaviours
- have the character apply 'odd' behaviours into their lives in a way which correlates to any moments of safety they felt during their traumatic experience (for instance, in *The Love Healer*, my hero, Emerson, inserts a screen between himself and his therapy clients, mimicking a moment of safety he felt during his trauma episode)
- recurring themes, symbols, and motifs (more on this soon)
- recurring words, scenes, sentences, and events

Example: Sieg was doing it again. Tightening the cravat at his neck. What *was* that about?

Scattered Narrative

Scattered narrative occurs when traumatic events are revealed in a piecemeal fashion. In other words, they are 'scattered' throughout the story. Think about one of your favourite fiction series: the story becomes more complete with each additional piece of description, right? That is scattered narrative. Applying this specifically to trauma, your readers will need to discover more about the trauma as the story unfolds.

Example: Jane Austen pulled the scattered narrative technique off in *Pride and Prejudice* when the reader, spoiler alert, learns about Georgiana Darcy's traumatic backstory with Mr Wickham later in the novel.

Note: this will be a harder technique to employ with success if you plan to use plotting methods such as *in media res*, where the reader learns about the trauma as it is happening.

Fragmentation/Fragmented Identity

As mentioned under the 'scattered narrative' subheading, trauma can be revealed in sections throughout the story. Though fragmentation is similar to the scattered narrative technique, scattered narratives tend to contain complete parts of the story scattered throughout, until a whole picture is formed. In comparison, when using fragmentation, writers can stop mid-way through an aspect of the trauma, then pick it up again later. It cuts apart the scattered narrative sections, showing only a portion. To give you a visual analogy, think about a jigsaw: the traumatic experience is the completed puzzle, each puzzle piece represents a scattered narrative leading to the whole, and cutting up an individual piece, then bringing those pieces together bit by bit, is fragmentation. This technique copies the fragmented identity trauma survivors may experience post-trauma.

Example: In slow motion, I saw the knife come to my throat, then – I heard myself scream. It woke me up.

Splitting the Narrative

This refers to intentionally dividing the narrative into different sections of time. For example, you might have multiple sections that dive into the past and others that are rooted in the present; a technique I utilised for *See Her Run*. You could also use the present-past-present technique — as I did in *The Love Healer*. The present-past-present technique is when you start your story in the present, then revert to the past to explain why the character is currently where they are, then conclude in the present to complete the story. Splitting the narrative mimics post-trauma effects, such as time frame disturbances and memory recall difficulties.

Surrealist Elements

You would be most likely to include surrealist elements in literary or magic realism trauma-themed subgenres — which is not to say you cannot use them in other subgenres! Basically, this refers to any surrealist elements which mimic the trauma or post-trauma effects in a symbolic, corresponding, or ethereal way. You could include dream sequences, fantasy sequences, seeming contradictions, the blurring of boundaries between what is real and what is not, and irrational/illogical parts.

Examples: check out any book by the Colombian writer and Nobel prize winner, Gabriel García Márquez (also known as 'Gabo' and 'Gabito') for inspiration. You could also take this opportunity to re-read *Alice's Adventures in Wonderland* by Lewis Carroll or even Virginia Woolf's *To the Lighthouse*. The main purpose of this technique is to highlight the 'derealised' and 'depersonalised' effects someone can experience post-trauma.

Voice Switching

Voice switching occurs when a writer changes from using active voice to passive voice, or vice versa. Switches in voice can be used to hint at trauma and/or its progression, as well as its lingering effects. For instance, the story can start with active voice (showing the character's self-confidence pre-trauma), switch to passive voice during/after a trauma (showing the disruption to self-confidence), then back to active once the character addresses their trauma experiences. Alternatively, passive voice (and dialogue) can be used when representing the trauma and active voice can be used at all other times, thereby putting the emphasis on the trauma.

Example of passive voice during the bank robbery: A ripple of something he wasn't ready to name was creeping up Sieg's spine. A robbery was taking place, and the question of what he was going to do about it hit him.

Example of active voice once Sieg is on his recovery journey: For the first time in months, I stood outside the bank. I braced for the usual dread to overtake me. But it didn't come.

Stream-of-Consciousness

According to writing craft author Jesse Matz, the 'stream-of-consciousness' style of writing is 'when writers let free associations run roughshod over the divisions and distinctions of standard punctuation'.

Example:
YES – you can use any form of punctuation you want!
and can even
use Not Proper Grammar   and sentence structure, to
get your point across.

What is your point, you might be asking? The point is to copy the disjointed, incohesive thoughts that can be a post-trauma effect. The stream-of-consciousness technique can intersect with the scattered narrative technique by having one topic (or part of the traumatic experience) lead into another in a somewhat free association style. In a similar vein, the split narrative technique can be used in conjunction with stream-of-consciousness since they can both add to the 'derealised' and 'depersonalised' experience of some trauma survivors. Using stream of consciousness means you are also less responsible for 'making sense', so it also works well with surrealist elements.

Other examples: Virginia Woolf is a fantastic author to read if you are looking to copy this style. A more specific book example is *As I Lay Dying* by William Faulkner.

Symbols and Motifs

Symbols and motifs can be used to hint at the trauma themes, the character arcs/ development, and as part of your repetition techniques. Some ways symbols and motifs can be used include:

- names
- weather
- setting/place
- furniture/decorations
- clothes/shoes

- Greek/Roman myths
- biblical references and myths
- other myths
- fairy tale allusions
- colours
- nature

Examples: in *See Her Run*, I gave my heroine a symbolic name: Diana King. It is a play on the name of the fictional superhero character Diana Prince — also known as *Wonder Woman*. The intention behind this name was to hint that my heroine would save herself (and those she loved) with her hidden inner strength. For a fantastic example of fairy tale allusions, check out Stephen King's book *Fairy Tale*, and see how many fairy tales you can deduce throughout. *The Color Purple* by Alice Walker shows you what a symbolic colour can do for a character (in this case, Celie) and their associated plot. Finally, in *The Love Healer*, I incorporated aspects of the Greek myth of Medea and Jason into the plot (for instance, when Emerson loses his shoe, in a nod to Jason's lost sandal).

As you can see, there are a multitude of ways to bring symbolism into your story; the above list is a starting point only. Of course, it is not necessary to include symbols at all, but they do add an underlying quality to your story that many readers will pick up, both consciously and subconsciously.

The Dual Voice Technique

The dual voice technique is used when a character says one thing but thinks something else. This technique can demonstrate the more private aspect of post-trauma effects, such as the mental grappling of conflicting thoughts and critical inner voices. To provide a more solid conceptualisation of this technique, here is a short example using Sieg:

> She asked me if I was okay.
> *No.*
> That's what I wanted to say.
> Instead, I muttered, 'Yes'.

This snippet shows Sieg's colleague asking if he is okay. Even though he thinks about saying 'no', he ultimately says 'yes'. The conflict between his private words and spoken words – his 'dual voice' — is clear even in this subtle form.

First-Person Point of View

I initially wrote *The Love Healer* in third-person point of view (POV), but quickly discovered the story, themes, and messages did not come across strongly enough. The third person failed to capture the lingering effects of the trauma. First person allowed a more personal interaction for myself as the writer and, I hope, the reader. It also made Neoma and Emerson's experiences feel more immediate and impactful. This is not to say that first person is an essential element of trauma-themed subgenres. Indeed, *See Her Run* is written in third-person point of view. My advice is to experiment; only you can know which POV works best.

First person example:	I felt terrified
Second person example:	You felt terrified
Third person example:	He felt terrified

You could also do something extra creative here and 'break the fourth wall': I felt terrified. You can probably sense it too, can't you?

Other Techniques

I am sure there are other techniques which will come to light the more people *intentionally* write trauma-themed subgenres. The provided information offers a place to start and does not claim to be the final word on this topic.

Blending the Two Methods

You can also use blended forms of the literary methods in concert with your plotting methods. For instance, your character might:
- engage in repetitive behaviours
- dissociate, depersonalise, and/or derealise (all three terms are defined in the glossary, towards the end of this book.)
- experience a fragmented memory

- experience a fragmented identity
- engage in interior monologues
- tell their story in parts

However, most of the above are advanced methods when it comes to representing trauma. Therefore, employ these techniques only if you feel confident and experienced enough to pull them off. You might also like to experiment with some of your own blended techniques.

Again, for the more visually inclined, Table 5 lists the complete plotting method and literary method techniques in a quick and easy reference guide.

The Plotting Method	The Literary Method
In media res/'in the middle of things'	Interior monologues
Flashbacks	Repetition/repetition compulsion
Dream/nightmare	Scattered narrative
Therapy	Fragmentation/fragmented identity
Conversation	Splitting the narrative
Gossip/rumours	Surrealist elements
Eavesdropping	Voice switching
The media	Stream-of-consciousness
	Symbols and motifs
	The dual voice technique
	First-person point of view
	Blended/other techniques

Table 5: The Plotting Methods and Literary Methods
Source: Author

Questions and Exercises

You can feel free to use the methods provided in Table 5, along with any other techniques you feel are appropriate, when answering these questions

1. What plotting methods might you use to represent trauma in your novel?
2. What plotting methods might you use to represent post-trauma effects in your novel (more on this in upcoming chapters)?
3. What literary methods might you use to represent trauma in your novel?
4. What literary methods might you use to represent post-trauma effects in your novel?
5. Would you consider any other methods?
6. Can you think of any blended methods?

Chapter 7 – Understanding Trauma Response

Before continuing, remember this: *all trauma-themed subgenres must contain an element of trauma representation, using plotting methods; you do not need to include trauma response* (or any other elements discussed from this point onwards). Even so, you might wish to read the following chapters to gain a broader understanding of trauma and learn more ways to use the plotting method. Further, you will need to keep reading if you want to create a more complex trauma-themed subgenre which includes trauma response, post-trauma effects, and post-trauma recovery. The more complex trauma-themed subgenres include anything post-trauma or transitional post-trauma.

Trauma Response Definition

The term 'trauma response' has a couple of meanings when it comes to trauma theory:

1. The initial response (or responses) to trauma — also known as the 'trauma reaction'
2. The possible lingering responses to trauma

This chapter deals primarily with the first meaning: the initial trauma response or responses. Subsequent chapters will look at the lingering responses. As can be surmised from the phrase, the initial trauma response happens to an individual at the time of the trauma.

The Role of the Autonomic Nervous System in Initial Trauma Response

During a traumatic situation, a series of (most likely) uncontrollable neurobiological-emotional events occur via the efficient — though it might not seem like it at the time — leadership of the autonomic nervous system (ANS). The ANS contains two major 'branches' known as the sympathetic nervous system (SNS) and parasympathetic nervous system (PNS).

Well-known trauma researcher Bessel Van der Kolk distinguishes between these branches by noting how the PNS acts as a brake while the SNS functions as the accelerator. You can use the following mnemonic memory tricks to help you remember the activities associated with each branch:

- P is for pause and the parasympathetic (in other words, pause equates to brake)
- S is for speed and the sympathetic (meaning, speed equates to accelerate)

Another way to recall the responsibilities of each branch is to think P for parasympathetic and:

- peace (feeling calm)
- procreation (hope this does not need an explanation!)
- pleasing (anything that feels good).

The parasympathetic governs these are activities. A more common, and crude, way to recall the responsibilities of the parasympathetic nervous system is as the rest-and-digest or breed-and-feed branch.

Similarly, for the sympathetic, you can remember S for sympathetic and:

- stress
- survival
- security

I prefer not to use the more common way of referring to this system as: fight or flight. This is because it can muddy understanding since trauma theorists use the terms when referring to specific trauma responses. Although the SNS *is* involved in trauma response, it is not necessarily interchangeable with the term, trauma response. For instance, the SNS activates during rapid eye movement (REM) dream states and high-intensity workouts. Most experts would not classify these examples as traumatic experiences — they might say they are instances of 'eustress' (i.e., good stress) — even though popular usage of the term 'traumatic' sometimes includes flippant usage such as, 'I found that workout *sooo* traumatising'. Therefore, to allay confusion, I do not support the use of 'fight or flight' when referring to the sympathetic nervous system. Instead, think speed.

The Initial Trauma Response Explained

Because the field of neuroscience and its trauma-related theory can become nuanced and complex, let's keep the explanation of initial trauma response very simple. I have devised the following dot points to describe the most accepted sequence of neurobiological-emotional events which are known to occur in the human organism during, and after, a traumatic experience:

- the *amygdala* (which receives sensory information and scans this information for potential hazards, risks, and dangers) senses a threat and alerts the hypothalamus.
- the *hypothalamus* (which processes information and sends messages from the brain to the body) sends a message to activate the sympathetic nervous system to prepare for possible action.
- the *sympathetic nervous system* responds by increasing blood pressure, breath rate, and heart rate, releasing cortisol and adrenalin/epinephrine, and shutting down bodily systems which require a lot of energy (such as digestion) to divert it to other systems that might need it more (such as the muscles).
- one or more *automatic initial trauma responses* are activated, leading to specific physiological, biological, emotional, and neurological behaviours and symptoms designed to bring the human being through the potentially threatening experience alive and safe.
- feedback obtained by *the brain* will either further agitate the SNS (which exacerbates the initial trauma responses and/or stimulates others), or rope in the PNS to take over and bring the individual back to a state of calm and regulation.
- the dominance of the SNS, and the corresponding extended or extreme interruption of the PNS, during a traumatic event can lead to specific, disturbing post-trauma effects.
- the brain, body, and nervous system's automatic attempts to overcorrect the interrupted PNS activation can show up as 'hypoarousal' post-trauma effects. If the SNS dominance was too strong, the brain and nervous system might not be able to override the activation, which is seen via 'hyperarousal' post-trauma states.

The basics of this information have been organised into Table 6 to guide further understanding.

Associated Parts	Associated Events
Amygdala	· Receives sensory information · Scans the sensory information for potential hazards, risks, and dangers · If it senses a threat, it alerts the hypothalamus
Hypothalamus	· processes information and sends messages from the brain to the body · sends a message to activate the sympathetic nervous system to prepare for possible action
Sympathetic nervous system	· Responds to the hypothalamus by increasing blood pressure, breath rate, and heart rate · Releases cortisol and adrenaline · Shuts down bodily systems requiring a lot of energy
Automatic initial trauma responses	· One or more initial trauma responses activated
Brain	· Agitates the SNS, or · Ropes in the PNS

Table 6: The Initial Trauma Response Explained
Source: Author

The 'BBANS'

glossary, towards the end of this book. Individuals <u>do not</u> survive terrible situations, as Dr Janina Fisher says, 'through thoughtful decision making or deliberate planning'. Rather, survival (probably) comes from automatic initial trauma responses. In other words, the brain, body, and nervous system (what I refer to as the BBANS) react to trauma in the way deemed most likely to result in survival of the human being. The reason I incorporated the words 'probably' and 'most likely' into the previous sentences is because, theoretically speaking, the pre-frontal cortex of the brain *could* override these innate neurobiological-emotional responses.

But (and it is a **big** but) this is highly improbable. Because, once threatening sensory input awakens the amygdala, the consequential rises in adrenalin and heart rate, and the shutting down of systems in the brain and body — in other words, the collective 'firing up' of the BBANS — makes overriding the response highly improbable. This is yet another reason 'blaming and shaming' a survivor for how they reacted to a traumatic event is pointless, unjust, and scientifically unsound. Initial trauma responses are involuntary, automatic, and beyond conscious control.

The Most Common Initial Trauma Responses

My PhD research enabled me to develop an original theoretical concept around initial trauma response. You can apply it to your trauma-themed subgenre as well. I named this concept the 'FAST' (Fear/Anxiety/Stress/Trauma) theory. It introduces the premise that any situation which invokes fear, anxiety, stress, or trauma responses, will result in certain symptoms and behaviours.

The symptoms and behaviours align with another concept I devised: the 8F Trauma Response Model (8FTRM). The 8Fs relate to eight English words beginning with an F. They derive from a variety of theories regarding 'typical' responses or reactions from individuals to fear/anxiety/stress/trauma. Hence, although the formulation of the 8F Trauma Response Model is my unique contribution to trauma theory, the concepts it is based on are not. You might find you are familiar with some of the terms in the 8FTRM, but your popular perception of these terms might differ from what you learn in the following pages. Remember, the information in this book is research-backed and accepted by most modern trauma theorists, so it does not necessarily align with the popular culture interpretations of these terms. This is what can set your book apart: authentic trauma and post-trauma representation.

The 8F Trauma Response Model

As mentioned, eight English words beginning with the letter F make up the 8FTRM. Before discussing each word in turn, it is important to remember that a human being (and, therefore, fictional character) does not need to have all the listed trauma responses during a traumatic episode, nor do they have to be experienced in the order presented. This is known as the 'non-linear response to trauma', meaning that everyone experiences the effects of trauma differently and/or not all the responses are encountered. All that is required is that the experience/s threatened an individual's feelings of safety and subsequent ideas of the self. They will experience that threat in at least one (usually more) of the ways described in Table 7 during their traumatic experience:

F word	Definition	Associated symptoms/behaviours
Flood	A potential threat is recognised, so the individual is flooded by powerful emotions.	Adrenaline rush, panic, overwhelming emotions and thoughts, heart rate and pulse rate spike.
Freeze	Stopping or limiting movement or being on guard/watchful/alert to gather information for next steps and prevent the likelihood of being spotted.	Hypervigilance, focused attention, scanning the environment, brain's logic centres shut down, pupils dilate, startle response inhibited, breathing slows.
Flight	Running away, fleeing, trying to escape a threatening situation.	Dry mouth, heart rate and blood pressure rise, somato-sensory perception lowers, breathing increases.
Fawn	Placating, appeasing, or submissive behaviour aimed towards stopping and/or preventing a perceived threat.	Being 'nice,' agreeing, doing whatever is asked, trying to 'be friends,' begging.
Fight	The urge to verbally and/or physically fight a perceived threat.	Flight symptoms increase, moving into a defensive stance or position.

Fright	Being unable to move (tonic immobility) and/or playing dead.	Feeling paralysed or unable to move, remaining still to imitate death.
Flag	Shutting down physically, mentally, and emotionally to limit possible pain perception and trauma.	Weak and flaccid muscles, emotional and physical numbness, language fails, derealisation, depersonalisation.
Faint	Dizziness, fuzzy-headedness, falling asleep, and/or fainting to limit possible pain perception and trauma.	Fainting, low blood pressure, cognitive failure, feeling unsteady, pain perception numbed, blacking out.

Table 7: The 8F Trauma Response Model
Source: Kindleysides 2024, p. 218

Read the table several times and think about your character/s. Do any of the responses seem natural to the character and their situation? Any you would like to experiment with writing? You will be able to ponder the possibilities some more in the questions and exercises section at the end of the chapter. Moreover, before moving on, you might want to consider the 9FTRM and the 'Fade' response.

The 9F Trauma Response Model and the Fade Response

My PhD research also posited the innovative inclusion of Fade — a previously unidentified ninth 'F word' — thus transforming the 8FTRM into the 9F Trauma Response Model (9FTRM). The Fade response can be defined as a strong desire to hide, be invisible, or disappear. Drawing on my PhD research, the behaviours and symptoms related to the Fade response include:

- trying to 'fade into the background'/make oneself 'invisible' or 'disappear'
- hiding/attempting to hide behind something/someone (or being shielded by someone)
- camouflaging/blending in attempts
- lowered or covered eyes
- lowered head
- hair/fringe covering the face and eyes
- contracted body language to appear smaller/invisible/less threatening
- crouching to appear smaller/invisible/less threatening

- wanting a hole to swallow them up
- making no sound
- making no movement
- hands/arms clasped/crossed in front of the body in a protective manner
- being on high alert
- holding the breath
- high heart rate (to allow for another response, if needed).

Taking this new proposed addition to trauma response into consideration, the 9Fs are: Flood, Freeze, Flight, Fawn, Fight, Fright, Flag, Faint, and Fade. Any of these initial trauma responses can, theoretically, be used as the basis for representing trauma response within your trauma plot ... but you may also want to consider how well (according to the research) the responses align with the trauma *type* you depict (I touched on trauma type in chapter 5). Though the next chapters discuss this topic in more detail, it is pertinent to remember that trauma type refers to whether the trauma is a 'once off' (acute) or 'prolonged/ multiple' (chronic) trauma. Keep that in the periphery of your mind and refrain from making a final decision around the initial trauma response/s until after you read the next few chapters.

Questions and Exercises

*You might like to refer to Table 7 while completing these questions and exercises:

1. Which initial trauma response/s would you like to explore in your novel? Note: this might change as you learn more throughout this book, but again, it is a good idea to jot down your intuitive insights first.
2. Write down some of the associated behaviours and symptoms from your chosen initial trauma response/s (by referring to Table 7).
3. Do you have any other ideas around how you would like to represent the initial trauma response/s? Add any instinctive ideas into your notebook or journal.
4. Is the traumatic experience a once-off event (acute) or prolonged (chronic)?

Chapter 8 – How to Represent the Initial Trauma Response in Your Fiction

Representing the initial trauma responses in your trauma-themed subgenre begins with describing a traumatic event — using any variety of plotting methods to reveal the trauma — then weaving one or more trauma responses into that description. Since I align with the experts who advocate for a non-linear trauma response, so you can feel free to pick any trauma responses which you think matches your character and their particular trauma. Subsequent chapters should make this easier to achieve since you will, hopefully, feel more confident in aligning trauma type (prolonged or short term/once-off) with the most likely trauma responses. Until then, how can you represent the initial trauma response in your fiction? You can use the plotting method and/or the literary method.

Representation Using the Plotting Method

The plotting method offers the simplest way to represent the initial trauma response. There are two basic ways to do this:

1. Use the provided definition of the trauma response.
   - Table 7 (plus Fade) in the previous chapter contains these definitions which you can use as a starting point for depicting the initial trauma response.
2. Use the provided symptoms and behaviours.
   - once again, Table 7 (plus Fade) in the previous chapter offers information on these.

You could choose one or both options depending on what you wish to achieve, the subgenre you have chosen (and whether trauma response is an essential characteristic to showcase in your plot), how confident you feel in representing these responses, and whether both options work together. When you make those decisions, write the trauma scenes and incorporate these associated responses from your character/s into the scene.

Let us use Sieg as an example here. You would provide the details of the bank robbery (thereby depicting the trauma) and weave in Sieg's responses to this trauma during the bank robbery (i.e., as it is happening). Hence, should you choose for Sieg to have a 'fright' response, you could have him, according to option 1 (definition), thinking about how he is unable to move: 'why can't I move'? Under option 2 (symptoms and behaviours), Sieg could remain physically still throughout the experience even though he might want to move: 'I tried to move my arm, but it was as if my body had filled with concrete'.

Sieg could also have a 'faint' response (more than one response is typical in 'real life', and according to current trauma theory, but you could technically rely on one major initial trauma response and still align with trauma theory). According to option 1 (definition) for the faint response, you might opt to depict Sieg as feeling dizzy: 'The robber took a step back, bringing me with them. The sensation of the steel at my neck made my head feel wobbly. God, don't let me faint!' For option 2 (symptoms and behaviours), you might decide to include a fainting scene: 'As soon as the thought came, my legs weakened. Oh-no...'

As you can see, depending on whether you use option 1 or option 2 (or both), the way the initial trauma response is represented will likely differ. How does the literary method contrast with these plotting methods?

Representation Using the Literary Method

A more complex way of representing the initial trauma response is through literary methods. Recall that this cannot be the only way you represent the initial trauma response — you must include plotting methods too. Continuing with the example used above, you could include words, sentences, paragraphs, and formatting within your writing which alludes to the freeze response. Consider this as an example:

I.

Could.

Not.

Move.

This layout slows the reading down, much like the freeze response slows the body down.

Likewise, you could depict the faint response like this:

I ...

    felt ...

        faint.

This layout provides a falling/dropping/fainting visual to the reader. Use your imagination and you never know what you can come up with. However, if this literary way seems too hard for you, it is fine to stick with the characterly method. The choice is up to you.

Of course, there are other ways you can represent the initial trauma response. Let us take a quick look at one of those now.

Another Idea

Another way for you to represent these initial trauma responses — but it is also harder and more challenging — is to show them occurring in other characters involved in the traumatic incident. Yes, you can depict other characters (even background, secondary, and minor characters) with these responses. They do not even have to be dramatic portrayals. Remember Sieg's colleague who was concerned about him and suggested therapy? She was also a hostage. Let us see her experience from Sieg's point of view (before he faints!): 'My gaze caught sight of something in my peripheral vision. Laura. She was edging closer to the secret alarm button set into the floor. If she managed to press it, the backup security would show up within two minutes'. Laura's initial trauma response could be 'fight' since she is attempting an activity to stop the robbery in this scene. Notice also that I showed this response in a couple of sentences. You do not need to draw it out (but you could, if it adds something substantial to your plot).

While adding reactions from other characters remains an option, if you do this, remember you must also depict at least one of your main characters experiencing an initial trauma response.

In trauma-themed fiction, trauma <u>must</u> be represented in at least one main character.

Important Representation Checklist

Below is a list of important checklist items to keep in mind when writing your initial trauma responses:

1. Stick to the facts (use the tables in this book)
2. Avoid relying on popular culture depictions of trauma response
3. Represent the traumatic event
4. Incorporate at least one initial trauma response in a main character into the traumatic event representation
5. No victim blaming or shaming. There is no 'right' initial trauma response.

Once you have completed the checklist, feel free to start the questions and exercises.

Questions and Exercises

1. Think about your chosen initial trauma responses. What ways can you depict this according to the option 1 plotting method (the definition from Table 7)?
2. Think about your chosen initial trauma responses. What ways can you depict this according to the option 2 plotting method (the symptoms and behaviours listed in Table 7)?
3. (Optional): How could you incorporate the initial trauma responses into the way you write the novel (the 'literary' methods)?
4. (Optional): How could you show initial trauma responses occurring in other characters involved in the traumatic event?
5. Have you complied with the checklist items?

Chapter 9 – Initial Trauma Responses as Post-Trauma Effects

Note: *adding post-trauma effects into your plot moves you into the transitional post-trauma and post-trauma subgenres.*

The Lingering Mode

Initial trauma responses are, probably, supposed to be temporary. However, the initial trauma response/s experienced by a human during a traumatic event sometimes linger/repeat in a kind of 'default' mode noted by Peter Levine. This default mode repeating from the initial trauma response equates to a 'post-trauma effect' — namely, those effects (symptoms and behaviours) experienced by an individual after a traumatic experience — since it continues post-trauma. Dr Sarah Woodhouse discusses the 'trauma loop' in what I view as a similar context and notes how 'the survival response can be momentary, but can continue indefinitely'. In addition, EMDR (Eye Movement Desensitisation and Reprocessing) originator Francine Shapiro refers to 'unprocessed memories' causing the 'feelings of danger' which are 'triggered by events in the present'. I refer to the continuance of the initial trauma responses as the 'lingering mode' since the initial trauma response lingers into the present.

As for who is most likely to suffer these lingering post-trauma effects, there is currently no identified trait which can aid therapists in detecting those most likely to experience post-trauma effects. In other words, it is not due to a failure of character, laziness, or 'hereditary predisposition' as was commonly suggested in psychotherapy's infancy. It *is* known, however, that the greater the severity, intensity, and duration of a traumatic experience, the greater the likelihood of post-trauma effects appearing in trauma survivors.

What else do we know about what causes the lingering mode to, well, linger and make post-trauma effects appear in an individual after the trauma is over (in the 'real world' at least)?

The short answer from some experts in the field seems to be that, according to the BBANS, the trauma is still happening *in the present moment* because a satisfactory ending to the traumatic event did not occur. Hence, the initial trauma responses continue to play out until the BBANS perceives that a satisfactory ending has happened. A satisfactory ending is one in which the BBANS feels the threat has been neutralised and the human organism is safe from further harm. This is the main theoretical reasoning behind why the trauma sometimes feels like it is still happening to trauma survivors in the present.

Can the Lingering Mode be Halted?

It is possible to achieve a satisfactory ending to the traumatic event (or a 'good enough' ending as many trauma experts say) hours, days, weeks, months, years, and decades post-trauma. This is achieved by employing certain methods discussed in upcoming sections and chapters. It is even possible to start the process immediately after the trauma has occurred (provided it is safe for the trauma survivor to engage in the required activities), as will soon be explained.

The reason an automatic resolution to trauma does not happen in some human beings, as it seems to in most other mammals, is up for debate and beyond an in-depth analysis in this book. Suffice to say, some experts, such as Peter Levine, believe the automatic rocking/shaking motions noted in animals after a traumatic encounter could hold a clue. The instinctual rocking/shaking movements of an animal post-trauma is something I have witnessed myself on many occasions. I live in a moderately-wooded suburb in Australia, with loads of native wildlife populating the area. Recently, a large, male, red kangaroo jumped out from the woods and bounced straight into the side of my car, despite the fact I had put the brakes on. I turned in my seat to check if he was okay, then watched while he shook his head/shoulders several times before bounding away, seemingly, unharmed. As such, I think there is definite credence to Levine's claims. Of course, this encounter could be a coincidence, however, at the very least, it is also intriguing enough to warrant further research.

Other trauma experts, such as Francine Shapiro, note the role of sleep, specifically REM states, in processing 'survival information', which might aid in settling trauma responses. Van der Kolk adds 'increasing our time in REM sleep reduces depression'. Hence, sleep, shaking, rocking, movement, and even swaying could all play a role in limiting post-trauma effects in humans in the immediate aftermath of a traumatic event. When it comes to those who come through trauma seemingly unaffected, it would be interesting to investigate whether they subconsciously engaged in any of these practices post-trauma. Here is another quick anecdote: knowing the possible benefits of shaking as-soon-as-is-safe after a traumatic event, I made the decision to engage in shaking after a recent, serious, life-saving surgery (I was warned beforehand that post-trauma effects were common and wanted to mitigate this). With obvious amusement, the nurses told me afterwards that I had begun shaking my feet and hands the instant I woke up from the anaesthesia ... but I do not remember doing it! Either way, I have not sustained any long-term post-trauma effects from this experience. Coincidence? Perhaps. Perhaps not. A definitive answer cannot be provided since sufficient research has not occurred in this space. For now, it is enough to know that, *sometimes*, sleep, shaking/rocking/swaying exercises, and general movement can *possibly* help to stave off post-trauma effects *if* employed as immediately as safely possible after a trauma (something to consider for your characters).

Many times, however, the trauma is not resolved in the BBANS, as evidenced by the hundreds of thousands, maybe even millions, of human beings suffering from some form of post-trauma effects.

As mentioned, the existence of post-trauma effects suggests the traumatic event is not finished according to the BBANS (which believes it is still happening) and, as a result, the BBANS also determines that the survivor still needs protection. Cue the initial trauma response as an attempt to correct this situation. If the post-trauma effects continue, so do the lingering trauma responses, in a continuous loop unless intentional efforts are made to delay or extend the loop timing. Moreover, other trauma responses not experienced during the original trauma can appear as post-trauma effects if the BBANS deem the initial trauma responses ineffective in creating safety and completing the traumatic event. This can also lead to other post-trauma effects (detailed in upcoming chapters).

What about Triggers?

Usually, the lingering mode (and dominant initial trauma response) becomes most apparent when a trauma survivor experiences a psychological 'trigger'. A trigger is 'something that reminds us of the original trauma' and 'sets off our traumatic reaction'. These quotes by Sarah Woodhouse show three connected aspects to triggers, namely:

1. Something happens
2. It reminds the trauma survivor of the original trauma in some way
3. This causes an automatic emotional, psychological, physical, and/or physiological response in the individual (which commonly aligns with the initial trauma responses experienced during the trauma, but not always).

Like the 3 main parts of the trauma definition used throughout this book (i.e., something happens, it threatens feelings of safety, and threatens ideas of the self), this three-part trigger definition will be important when it comes to portraying a triggered character in your book. Let us apply it to Sieg:

1. He sees a butcher pick up a knife at the local grocery store (something happens)
2. It flashes a memory of the knife held to his throat in the bank robbery (reminds him of the trauma)
3. He has a panic attack (automatic response)

You will need to use the same three basic elements in your own representation — if you include triggers in your manuscript, of course. As an important aside before continuing, the term 'trigger' is another concept co-opted in the popular imagination, with trivial occurrences being assigned the status of a trigger even when a typical, expected response happens, such as getting upset if someone steals your car park. In trauma theory, a trigger is not something trivial, therefore it should not be used lightly in your novels (or real-life). According to trauma theory, a genuine trigger must contain the above three aspects.

To demonstrate these concepts as they correspond to specific initial trauma responses, consider this: if one of the initial responses during your character's trauma experience is 'fight' then the character might respond to another possible threat which reminds them of the original trauma (a trigger) in 'fight mode'. As Dr Sarah Woodhouse notes, 'We embody aspects of who we were at the time of the initial experience'. Research Professor MaryCatherine McDonald adds, 'When you are exposed to a trigger, your brain and body cannot tell the difference between the present and the past'. This shows how the BBANS believes it is experiencing the original trauma and still needs to protect itself by repeating the initial trauma response to achieve a satisfactory ending.

Further to this, triggers can come from any of the main senses — smell, sight, touch, sound, taste — which might have been activated during the trauma. For instance, think about whether your character would have noticed a distinct smell during the trauma (e.g., the smell of rust on the knife or the smell of blood if Sieg's throat is nicked), a unique sound (e.g., a knife being pulled from its sharpening pouch), a taste (e.g., salty sweat dripping down Sieg's face and sliding into his mouth), sight (e.g., several people holding knives), and touch (e.g., the sensation of the robber grabbing Sieg). All of these sense-related trauma details hold the potential for creating character trauma triggers in your novel. Use your imagination when it comes to this, and you might be pleasantly surprised by what you come up with.

To reiterate, writers can choose to rely solely on the initial trauma responses, and apply the associated symptoms and behaviours mentioned in Table 7, as their characters' corresponding post-trauma effects due to triggers. This is an acceptable decision according to current research, as is combing the lingering mode with other post-trauma effects (detailed in the next chapter).

If you choose to adopt the lingering mode post-trauma effect in your novel, you will need to represent the associated symptoms and behaviours in your character (outlined in Table 7) after the character is triggered. As you did for the initial trauma response, you can again use the information in Table 7 for inspiration around ways to represent the lingering mode in your character/s. The difference is: you will also need to include a trigger which causes the lingering mode trauma response. The questions and exercises section can help you refine your ideas around this.

Questions and Exercises

Table 7 can aid you in answering these questions

1. Will you consider using the lingering/default mode as a post-trauma effect? Why/why not?
2. If so, what was/were the initial trauma response/s you chose for your character/s?
3. What are the corresponding behaviours and symptoms?
4. These behaviours and symptoms need to appear in your character/s as a result of triggers which resemble or remind the character/s of the trauma experience. What triggers can you include in your story (including sense-related triggers)?
5. Drawing upon the noted symptoms and behaviours you listed above, how will your character/s respond to the triggers?

Chapter 10 – What Are Some of the Other Post-Trauma Effects?

Once again, the question of 'other post-trauma effects' is a contested space in academia. For example, Alan Gibbs (as stated in Tamas Bényei and Alexandra Stara's work) claims there can be no agreement on universal post-trauma symptoms as this 'devalues' the individual experience of trauma. Gibbs' perspective opens the trauma experience in the same way as the 9FTRM and personalises the experience by noting how an individual can have any of these experiences as opposed to a linear, prescribed response. Dr Janina Fisher refers to the post-trauma effects of trauma as a 'living legacy', meaning survivors are left to deal with a 'legacy' from the original trauma that seems to take on a life of its own. In the same vein as Gibbs, according to Fisher, this legacy is individual and can manifest in many ways.

These opinions not only confirm that the initial trauma responses can linger and become post-trauma effects, but also that other post-trauma effects are possible. As such, drawing upon my previously offered definition of trauma, and adding the concept of post-trauma effects, the definition becomes 'an experience/s which threatens feelings of safety and subsequent ideas of the self *and leads to unpleasant symptoms* following the experience'. This corresponds with the definitions provided by Gibbs and Fisher, including leaving the precise symptoms related to post-trauma effects open-ended. To allay confusion over what I mean by 'unpleasant', in this context, the word refers to whatever the individual identifies as unwanted or intrusive. I also advocate for the view that the individual person (or, in this context, your character) can experience any of the 9Fs and/or any of the other post-trauma effects discussed in turn below. Therefore, whether you decide to incorporate any of these post-trauma effects into your novel is a personal choice (as well as dependent upon your chosen subgenre).

When reading through the following post-trauma effects, remember I am providing a brief overview only. It should also be noted that I am not suggesting these are the only possible post-trauma effects. However, they are the effects recorded most often in the research, which is why they are my focus. Some of these may be familiar to you whilst others might be new. Do not skip past the familiar post-trauma effects because, sometimes, the popular conception of these differs to what the research and respected experts say.

Characters May Experience PTSD or CPTSD/PTSR or CPTSR

Even though most of you probably already know, for those who might not, these acronyms stand for: post-traumatic stress disorder (PTSD) and complex post-traumatic stress disorder (CPTSD). Before continuing, I want to note here that PTSD and CPTSD are *normal* reactions to trauma, therefore, the only 'disorder' relevant to these post-trauma effects relates to the dysregulated/disordered nervous system. Hence, the acronyms PTSR and CPTSR — meaning Post-Traumatic Stress Reaction and Complex Post-Traumatic Stress Reaction, respectively — are used from this point forward. These acronyms could also be used as a discussion point in your novel should you choose to dive deeper into this. For instance, you could have one character say, 'Was that a PTSD symptom?' and you could have the trauma survivor character explain they prefer the use of the term 'PTSR' for the above reasons. Or, you can use PTSD (I have in some of my articles and fiction).

Even though both conditions result in intrusive effects, PTSR is probably the most publicly well-known trauma effect whereas CPTSR is not. According to the *DSM 5* — *the Diagnostic and Statistical Manual, Version 5* (the pre-eminent book advocated by the American Psychiatric Association and used by many psychiatrists to diagnose mental health issues) — PTSR is 'the development of characteristic symptoms following exposure to one or more traumatic events'. The characteristic symptoms can include:

- intrusive memories of the trauma
- nightmares
- flashbacks
- loss of awareness of present surroundings (dissociation)
- feeling detached from the self/body (depersonalisation)
- distress after exposure to traumatic triggers (anything that reminds the

individual of the trauma)

- avoidance of trauma-related memories and triggers
- negative self-beliefs/views of the world/emotional states
- loss of interest in formerly loved activities
- feelings of detachment from others
- inability to experience positive emotions
- irritability
- angry outbursts
- reckless/self-destructive behaviour (this can appear in the form of negative coping and defence mechanisms)
- an exaggerated startle response

In comparison, CPTSR is defined by Dr Arielle Schwartz as post-trauma symptoms 'which occurs as a result of long-term exposure to traumatic stress'. Lucy Bond and Stef Craps also note the 'prolonged, repeated trauma' in CPTSR trauma survivors. Bessel van der Kolk concurs, saying CPTSR can develop in those individuals with 'histories of prolonged and severe interpersonal abuse'. Weixi Wang and colleagues concur that CPTSR is 'derived from inescapable, prolonged exposure to trauma'. CPTSR researcher Michael Thompson also agrees, noting that CPTSR 'develops after prolonged or repeated exposure to trauma'. Therefore, along with the common PTSR symptoms, CPTSR can include:

- avoidance behaviours
- emotional flashbacks
- disturbing physical sensations
- emotional/affect dysregulation
- negative self-concept
- relationship disturbances
- toxic/chronic shame/guilt
- dissociation
- numbness
- worthlessness
- a more negative inner critic
- social anxiety
- hypervigilance

- depressive symptoms
- a multitude of physical health problems

Though CPTSR is not yet (as of writing this book) officially recognised in the *DSM 5*, the World Health Organization does recognise the condition, stating on their International Classification of Diseases website that it can occur 'following exposure to an event or series of events of an extremely threatening or horrific nature, most commonly prolonged or repetitive events from which escape is difficult or impossible'.

Despite the conditions sharing many of the same symptoms, as seen from the definitions given, PTSR typically occurs after one or more short-term (acute) traumatic experiences whereas CPTSR commonly presents after multiple, prolonged, inescapable, repeated, or long-term (chronic) traumatic events. In case you have missed the connection to information I sign-posted earlier, this is the point where these so-called 'disorders' intersect with the ideas around 'trauma type'. Should you choose to represent PTSR or CPTSR in your novel as a post-trauma effect in your character/s, you might want to ensure the chosen traumatic event aligns with this post-trauma effect. In other words, do you portray a once-off event, like a bank robbery, with PTSR post-trauma effects? Alternatively, do you portray a childhood survivor of parental drug addiction with CPTSR post-trauma effects? Or, do you go for something more complex: such as how I have shown Sieg experiencing hyperaroused symptoms after a once-off event (that the reader is aware of, since the idea for this example story is that Sieg has had other traumas) despite hyperarousal commonly — but <u>not</u> exclusively — being associated with multiple or prolonged trauma?

Take the opportunity now to go back over the notes you have made for the chosen trauma event and ensure it aligns with this new information. If it does not, you do not need to panic and change your entire story idea. The worlds of trauma theory and literary trauma theory — where literary studies and trauma studies intertwine — support any of the 9Fs, and the other post-trauma effects outlined in this chapter, as accepted theoretical post-trauma effects *regardless of the applicability of chronic or acute trauma type*. Indeed, as you have likely noticed, the symptoms sometimes crossover. However, if you really want to nail the research-backed aspect of your novel, you may want to consider re-evaluating during the questions and exercises at the end of this chapter. That being said, let me make it explicitly clear that it is also acceptable if you choose not to align your story and trauma plot with the concept of trauma type.

The following post-trauma effects, hypovigilance and hypervigilance, also link to PTSR and CPTSR and trauma types. Since these ideas, and the way they connect, can get confusing at this stage, I have also included Table 8 (after the next subheading) to assist in aiding you to understand their connections in a more visual way.

Characters May Experience Hypervigilance or Hypovigilance/ Hyperarousal or Hypoarousal

For the purposes of this book, the terms hypervigilance and hypovigilance are used interchangeably with the terms hyperarousal and hypoarousal. Hypoarousal responses during a traumatic event have been recorded in studies as being a high indicator for subsequent PTSR development. Based on that research, I contended in my PhD thesis that hyperarousal responses could equally be a high indicator for CPTSR development. That hypothesis is taken for granted from this point onwards (but is still up for debate).

According to Maggie Schauer and Thomas Elbert, 'dissociative PTSR' (PTSR effects that align with hypoarousal/hypovigilant responses) is defined by 'physiological adaptations, including immobility, pain tolerance and with it "switches" in consciousness, information processing, and behavior'. Based on these distinctions, the lingering fright, faint, and flag trauma responses align with the 'hypoarousal' category. Since a definition of CPTSR can be delineated from the PTSR definition, CPTSR could be defined by physiological adaptions, including running and being on high alert, alongside 'switches' in consciousness, information processing, and behaviour. That being the case, the flood, freeze, flight, fight, fawn responses (and, as mentioned in my PhD, I suspect the Fade response) and CPTSR effects correspond with the 'hyperarousal' category.

To simplify further:
- Hyperarousal could be defined by physiological adaptations which align with the lingering flood, freeze, flight, fight, fawn, and fade trauma responses, and sometimes results in common CPTSR effects.

- Hypoarousal could be defined by physiological adaptations which align with the lingering fright, faint, and flag trauma responses, and sometimes results in common PTSR effects.

Even though the above information seems to signal a simple split between hypovigilance and hypervigilance, according to Levine, most trauma survivors experience both hypervigilant and hypovigilant symptoms to some degree, but it is the expression of these symptoms which differs. This is another reason I mention that it is fine to incorporate any of the suggested post-trauma effects. One-size does not fit-all when it comes to the after-effects of trauma.

With that proviso in mind, Table 8 contains a more concise, visual categorisation of these two post-trauma effects and the way they intersect with PTSR, CPTSR, trauma type, and initial trauma responses. Note here that the list of initial trauma responses (i.e., the 8FTRM and 9FTRM) proffered in Table 7 also align with the 'lingering mode' version of initial trauma responses, hence, you can technically match the corresponding symptoms/behaviours with post-trauma effects in your novel.

Further to this, keep in mind that Table 8 is not intended to be exhaustive and is also not entirely my original contribution (except for the addition of the 'Fade' response/symptoms), with others having coined these terms and made their own lists, tables, and figures before now. However, I synthesised the contributions of others and made the research accessible to other writers through the compilation of this table.

	Hypoarousal/Hypovigilance	Hyperarousal/Hypervigilance
Nervous system involvement	Parasympathetic nervous system overactivation (or, sympathetic nervous system under-activation)	Sympathetic nervous system overactivation.
Trauma type	Acute. Commonly seen in one-off trauma events.	Chronic. Commonly seen in long-term trauma events.
Initial trauma responses	Fright, faint, and flag.	Fright, flood, freeze, flight, fight, fawn, and fade.

Associated post-trauma condition	PTSR	CPTSR (proposed)
Associated post-trauma effects	Low arousal, evading, avoiding, emotionally numb/unable to 'feel feelings,' feeling 'shut down' or 'not present,' passivity, lack of energy, foggy thoughts/ unable to think, feeling disconnected, dissociation, derealisation, depersonalisation, shame/ guilt, inability to say 'no,' denial, repression, depression, despair, hopelessness, shame, feeling unworthy, memory loss.	High arousal, racing thoughts, hypersensitivity, anxiety, aggression, irritability, overwhelm, emotional dysregulation, panic, flashbacks, intrusive memories, impulsiveness, nightmares, hypervigilance, jumpiness, stiff posture, defensiveness, sudden anger/ outbursts, reactivity, feeling unsafe, elevated stress hormones, high blood pressure and heart rate.

Table 8: Two ways for authors to represent post-trauma effects
Source: Adapted from Kindleysides 2024, p. 226

As Table 8 demonstrates, many post-trauma effects can be categorised as 'dualities' or 'opposites'. When you make a final decision, during the questions and exercises at the end of this chapter, about the post-trauma effects to allocate to your character/s, it can prove helpful to decide whether the character is mostly 'hyperaroused' or 'hypoaroused'. Again, this is a personal choice. So long as you choose at least one post-trauma effect to portray, you will align with the current research. To clarify even more, you can choose from the following post-trauma effects and still be in line with current research:

1. A lingering mode from the initial 9F trauma responses
2. PTSR or CPTSR
3. Hypoarousal or hyperarousal
4. PTSR, hypoarousal, the acute trauma type, and the fright, faint, and flag trauma responses

5. CPTSR, hyperarousal, the chronic trauma type, and the fright, flood, freeze, flight, fight, fawn, and fade trauma responses
6. Any combination of the above.

As you can see, the most recent research gives you plenty of options. Some other post-trauma effects you can also consider representing (either independently or alongside those mentioned above, depending on the necessary characteristics of your chosen subgenre) are detailed next.

Characters May Experience Coping Mechanisms and/or Defence Mechanisms

The terms 'coping mechanism' and 'defence mechanism' can be defined in various ways, with some theorists arguing that no differences exist between the two. Even so, I align with those theorists who separate the two.

Through my PhD research, I was able to define coping mechanisms in the context of trauma as (mostly) 'conscious' — that is, what a person is aware of — strategies used by trauma survivors to help them cope with the lasting effects of trauma. Survivors are usually aware/conscious of the coping mechanism and its intended purpose (but not always: there are always exceptions in trauma theory). Coping mechanisms can be positive or negative, and even neutral, but are most commonly negative. Some examples of negative coping mechanisms include:

- drug use
- alcohol abuse
- promiscuity (no 'slut shaming')
- eating disorders
- self-harm
- risk-taking
- gambling
- porn addiction
- other addictions.

As can be surmised from this list, coping mechanisms often appear as a physical (outer) manifestation of trauma.

In contrast, I define defence mechanisms in the context of trauma as 'unconscious' — that is, what a person is not aware of — strategies used by trauma survivors to protect, repress, or defend against trauma and its effects. This aligns with Sigmund Freud's own definition of defence mechanisms: 'individuals used various strategies meant to repress, change, or keep away harmful thoughts'. As discussed under the PTSR/CPTSR heading, trauma survivors commonly experience 'harmful thoughts' as a post-trauma effect. Defence mechanisms are, therefore, usually unconscious inner mental strategies used by survivors. Once again, these can be positive, neutral, or negative. Some examples of negative defence mechanisms include:

- keeping others at a distance
- 'building walls' (the psychological, emotional, mental, and relational kind)
- being cold
- aloofness
- preferring to be alone
- repressing memories
- socially isolating
- withdrawal
- trying not to appear 'weak'

Thus, defence mechanisms, being unconscious, tend towards more mental and emotional (inner) manifestations of trauma.

Furthermore, since there can be considerable overlap in symptoms, as already mentioned according to Levine, writers can scatter aspects of the other, non-dominant mechanism into their plots and still align with current research.

Take a moment to pause and think about the coping and defence mechanisms described. Do you think they could apply to your story? You do not necessarily need to include them in your chosen subgenre, but they can definitely add something extra to your plot. Having said that, including them also complicates your writing, so you need to be honest as to whether you feel up to the task of writing them.

Drug and alcohol abuse is important to expound upon at this point since substance abuse as a coping mechanism has a high correlation in trauma survivors. Like the defence and coping mechanisms, incorporating a drug and/or alcohol abuse subplot into your story can increase both the difficulty of writing your novel in an authentic, research-backed way as well as add an extra layer of depth to the plot. Only you can decide whether or not you think you can attempt this. If you do, remember the ethical considerations discussed in Chapter 1 around accurate representation being necessary to avoid retraumatisation in your readers.

Characters May Experience Shame or Guilt

Well-known shame researcher, Brené Brown, says shame is an 'intensely painful feeling' and that it feels like 'something we've experienced, done, or failed to do makes us unworthy of connection'. Brown defines guilt as, 'Holding something we've done or failed to do up against our values and feeling psychological discomfort'. Put simply, shame relates to negative feelings we have of ourselves based on something that has happened to us, whereas guilt relates to negative feelings we have of ourselves based on something we have done (or perceive we have done). Arielle Schwartz also lists chronic shame as one of the symptoms of CPTSR. Hence, depicting guilt and shame can be good options when it comes to post-trauma effects. Personally, I think every trauma plot, regardless of subgenre, should have an aspect of shame or guilt in the characters. Therefore, this might be another layer of your plot to adapt.

Characters May Experience Retraumatisation

Even though this concept has been overviewed in earlier chapters, I wanted to highlight a connection that some readers might have missed: retraumatisation can lead to post-trauma effects. For a refresher, retraumatisation is 'a trauma survivor being exposed to situations which force them to relive their traumatic experiences'. As my definition alludes, retraumatisation is typically caused by a trigger — something that reminds the survivor of the original trauma — which sometimes results in associated post-trauma effects. These post-trauma effects commonly align with the trigger and the way it relates to the trauma. For instance, using the ongoing example, if your character survived a bank robbery, being in a line at the bank could cause them to 'relive' the experience. This could result in intrusive flashbacks or other unwanted effects. You might wish to show your characters experiencing retraumatisation to add another interesting layer into your trauma representation.

Characters May Experience Depression

Depression is a common comorbid — meaning, it appears alongside other symptoms — post-trauma effect. Despite depictions in popular culture, depression is actually a multi-faceted and complex condition with a variety of subtypes and specific diagnoses under the 'mood disorder' umbrella. As such, please take care when portraying depression and depressive symptoms in your work. Make sure you familiarise yourself with the particulars of depression before taking it on. Common symptoms include, but are not limited to, extended periods of sadness and/or hopelessness, and loss of interest in formerly enjoyed activities. As always: remember to keep the portrayal accurate, sensitive, and fact-based by researching specific depressive disorders.

Characters May Experience a Decline in Physical Health

Physical health fallout is another well-documented — and shocking, once you know the full extent — post-trauma effect. Below is a list of some of the conditions with a known association with trauma. You might want to portray one, some, or none of them. Again, if you choose this option: research the facts, stick to the facts, and portray it with authenticity, accuracy, and sensitivity. Remove victim blaming and shaming.

1. Chronic Pain

   - muscle tension, headaches/migraines, and fibromyalgia.

2. Cancer (yes, really)

   - breast, colorectal, lung, esophageal, cervical, prostate, pancreatic, and skin.

3. Sleep Disturbances

   - insomnia, persistent nightmares/night terrors, and sleep apnea.

4. Digestive Disturbances

- irritable Bowel Syndrome (IBS), nausea, loss of appetite (see also weight disturbances), and acid reflux/heartburn.

5. Cardiovascular Issues

- hypertension, heart disease, and heart palpitations.

6. Immune System Issues

- frequent illnesses (such as colds and flus) and autoimmune conditions.

7. Weight Disturbances (please exercise extreme caution if choosing this option, due to the seriousness of eating disorders)

- either weight loss or weight gain.

8. Skin and Hair Issues

- eczema/psoriasis/stress rashes, acne, and hair loss/thinning.

9. Musculoskeletal Issues

- joint pain (especially in the knees, hips, and wrists), arthritis, and back pain.

Since there are a lot of other post-trauma effects to reflect on, Table 9 provides a handy summary for you to refer to when needed.

Other Post-Trauma Effect	Brief Definition or Overview
PTSD/PTSR	Associated with once-off traumatic events, commonly with hypoarousal symptoms
CPTSD/CPTSR	Associated with prolonged or multiple traumatic events, commonly with hyperarousal symptoms
Hypervigilance/Hyperarousal	Associated with high arousal symptoms (e.g., racing thoughts, hypersensitivity, and anxiety)
Hypovigilance/Hypoarousal	Associated with low arousal symptoms (e.g., numbing, evading, and avoiding)

Coping Mechanisms	Conscious strategies used by trauma survivors to help them cope with the lasting effects of trauma
Defence Mechanisms	Unconscious strategies used by trauma survivors to protect, repress, or defend against the lasting effects of trauma
Shame	Negative feelings we have of ourselves based on something that has happened to us
Guilt	Negative feelings we have of ourselves based on something we have done (or perceive we have done)
Retraumatisation	When a trauma survivor is exposed to situations which force them to relive their traumatic experiences
Depression	An umbrella term for a group of mood disorders characterised by prolonged periods of sadness and/or hopelessness, and loss of interest in formerly enjoyed activities
Decline in Physical Health	Conditions can include: chronic pain, cancer, sleep issues, digestive issues, cardiovascular issues, immune system issues, weight issues, skin/hair issues, and musculoskeletal issues

Table 9: Other Post-Trauma Effects
Source: Author

This chapter aimed to show you the variety of post-trauma effects open to you to represent as a trauma-informed writer. Did any of these post-trauma effects surprise you? Maybe they will surprise and, therefore, inform your readers too?

Questions and Exercises

This chapter provided a lot of information (it is one of the longest in the book). If you need to, feel free to re-read it and peruse Table 8 again to lock the ideas into your brain. Then, come back and complete these exercises.

1. What is the 'trauma type' you plan on depicting in your novel: a one-off (acute) or prolonged (chronic) trauma? Does this remain unchanged from when you first answered this question?

2. According to the trauma responses you chose for your character, are they more likely to be on the hyperaroused (CPTSR) or hypoaroused (PTSR) spectrum?

3. How could you represent these symptoms and behaviours in your novel?

4. Would your character be likely to experience defence mechanisms or coping mechanisms? Both?

5. How could you represent the chosen defence or coping mechanisms in your novel?

6. Would your character be likely to experience shame or guilt?

7. How could you represent shame and/or guilt in your novel?

8. Would your character/s be likely to experience drug or alcohol abuse?

9. How could you represent the drug/alcohol in your novel?

10. Would your character be likely to experience post-trauma effects from retraumatisation?

11. How could you represent the retraumatisation and its post-trauma effects in your novel?

12. Would your character be likely to experience depression? How will you portray this?

13. Would your character be likely to have physical fallout? What would this be?

Chapter 11 – How to Represent the Other Post-Trauma Effects in Your Fiction

Like with trauma representation, initial trauma response representation, and lingering mode representation, writers must have a basic knowledge of the other post-trauma effects to represent them effectively in their works. That is why the previous chapter was necessary to read before moving onto this topic, especially considering the complexity of the topic (the previous chapter is one of the longest in this book). When it comes to specific ways to represent the other post-trauma effects, once again, trauma theorists (approaching the topic from different fields, including psychology and literature) disagree on the best approach. This muddies a simple approach to the other post-trauma effect representation. Even so, by drawing upon theory, and applying the suggestions given previously, it is possible to devise a workable solution.

For instance, you can represent the other post-trauma effects in your novel in the same two easy ways you used for representing the initial trauma response, namely:

1. Use the provided definition of the post-trauma effect in the previous chapter (and shown in Table 9) to check if it matches with the proposed traumatic experience type (is it chronic or acute?).

2. Use the provided symptoms and behaviours in the previous chapter (and shown in Table 9) as a starting point for ideas on representation.

Employing Sieg as an example, you could choose for him to have PTSR-related post-trauma effects. The provided definition of PTSR is post-trauma symptoms which typically occur after one (sometimes more) short-term (acute) traumatic experiences. According to this definition, then, the PTSR choice gels well with current research since a bank robbery is a once-off (hopefully) event for the character. With the PTSR/trauma type choice made, you can then choose option 1, option 2, or both in writing. Remember, you cannot write 'the character had PTSR because of the once-off event of the bank robbery' (unless you are writing a background trauma novel). You also need to represent the PTSR post-trauma effects when choosing to write in the post-trauma and, possibly, the transitional post-trauma subgenres. This is where option 2 picks up the slack.

By looking at the PTSR symptomology given in Table 8, you can see some of these symptoms on the list: low arousal, evading, avoiding, emotionally numb/unable to 'feel feelings', feeling 'shut down' or 'not present'. Therefore, you could represent your trauma survivor character/s avoiding people/places/situations, not reacting to joyful experiences the way they once would have, and disconnecting from their lives.

On the other hand, if you chose for the character to display hypovigilant/hypoaroused post-trauma effects (which corresponds with PTSR as per Table 8), you would first look at the definition: defined by physiological adaptations which align with the lingering fright, faint, and flag trauma responses. Then, you could check if the character/s have responded during the trauma with one of these responses. In the example I gave of a bank robbery, I had Sieg respond with the 'fright' and 'faint' initial trauma response, both of which correspond to the research on hypoarousal/PTSR post-trauma effects. With this aligned, you can bring in option 2 by looking at the associated behaviours and symptomology around fright and faint from Table 7. Two of these include low blood pressure and cognitive failure. Therefore, you can represent your character with the physiological consequences of low blood pressure, such as: feeling weak, tired, or dizzy. Or, if you choose to represent cognitive failure, you could show the character having trouble with their memory, thinking, and concentrating. As you can see, there are lots of available choices.

Like the initial trauma response representation, another (harder) way for you to represent the post-trauma effects is to show them occurring in other characters involved in the trauma. However, if you do this, remember you must also depict at least one of your main characters experiencing post-trauma effects (if you are writing in the post-trauma subgenres).

A Warning About Stereotypes

Any type of stereotype in writing should be avoided, and it is no different when it comes to representing post-trauma effects. You can avoid this, again, by sticking to the facts, doing the research, becoming trauma-informed, and cross-referencing with the included tables in this book.

Questions and Exercises

1. Refer to the definitions of post-trauma effects you jotted down during the exercises in the previous chapter. Which align the best with your chosen traumatic experience?
2. Which would you like to use in your novel?
3. Refer to Tables 8 and 9 to double-check your post-trauma effects symptoms and behaviours align with the representation you plan to incorporate into your manuscript.
4. How will you represent the post-trauma effects in your characters? Feel free to refer to any notes you made during the exercises in the previous chapter, and in Tables 8 and 9.

Chapter 12 – How Do Post-Trauma Effects Impact Romantic Relationships?

Before reading this chapter, please note: *if you write in the post-trauma romance subgenre, you* <u>*must*</u> *represent post-trauma effects impacting on the romantic relationship/s.* Other subgenres have some flexibility with this element. Even so, post-trauma effects can, and do, interfere with non-intimate relationships as well (and this can be shown in any trauma-themed subgenre). The next chapter addresses the impact of trauma on non-intimate relationships. Both this chapter and the following chapter can also assist in building your relationship arc.

Trauma can impact all of a survivor's relationships; this includes family, work colleagues, friendships, business partnerships, *and* romantic relationships. Depending on the subgenre you are writing, you might choose to depict all of these relationship impacts, none, or focus only on the romantic relationship/s. The more relationships you choose to represent as impacted, the more difficult your novel will be to write. However, this is accurate according to research — every relationship a trauma survivor had before the traumatic event is likely to be impacted after the event, as are future/new relationships. Even so, you can still choose to narrow in on the impact on the romantic relationship/s only.

Potential Impact Areas

What is meant by 'impact'? To keep it simple, I mean anything that changes the dynamics of the romantic relationship. Impacts can be classed as minor and major. For established romantic relationships, most often the impact revolves around the trauma survivors' new behaviours and symptoms, and how this affects the partner/s (if you are writing polyamorous, love triangle, ménage, and so on plots, you will need to consider all the love interests and whether you will write about the impacts on one or all of them). For instance, if your traumatised character lavished their lover/s with physical touch before the trauma, but avoids it after the trauma, this can affect the partner/s.

You can show the love interest/s reacting to this changed behaviour and symptomology in positive, negative, or neutral ways. Basic examples demonstrating these reactions are:

- a partner 'steps up' by offering support and understanding (positive)
- a partner reacts with anger (negative)
- a partner reacts as though nothing has happened (neutral, but can also be negative depending on how this reaction affects the traumatised character)

These reactions serve as an opportunity not only to depict this important fallout from trauma but also to provide an opportunity to develop conflict within the plot (and add some unexpected antagonists or cheerleaders).

Another important aspect, hinted at in the examples above, is to consider how the trauma survivor reacts/thinks/feels about the love interests, and the reaction the love interests are having to them. Are the trauma survivors upset with the partner/s who do not seem to understand (they most likely would be)? Are they surprised by their love interest stepping up? Do they feel guilty about 'not pulling their weight' in the relationship since the trauma? Do they push their partner/s away? Do they shun intimacy? Alternatively, have they become hyper-intimate (though not often shown in popular culture, hypersexuality after sexual trauma is a possible post-trauma effect)? Again, this is a great site for exploring the post-trauma fallout as well as create interesting subplots, conflict, and potential for 'post-traumatic growth' (discussed in an upcoming chapter).

Something else to consider is the stage of the romantic relationship. A new/blossoming/burgeoning relationship will be impacted differently to one established pre-trauma. For example, if you are using a 'friends-to-lovers' trope, the love interests could have known each other for years. This would be written differently to 'friendship formed due to being in the bank robbery together' and it later developing into a romantic situation. In another scenario, one of the love interests could be the sister of one of the other bank robbery survivors (loads of other romantic plots/subplots could be developed from this bank robbery storyline as well).

Each of these options will also have different power and relationship dynamics that can impact on the developing romance. Will power dynamics need to be renegotiated? Were they ever negotiated? What about relationship dynamics (consider: who does what, what are the expected roles and responsibilities of each partner)? How will these change?

Relationship structures could also change due to trauma. Think: commitment, monogamy, consensual non-monogamy, polyamory, open, and other relationship structures. Will your characters need to have conversations around the restructuring of their relationships? Could it lead to a break up or renewed/changed level of commitment? As this overview shows, there is a lot to consider when it comes to romantic relationship impact post-trauma.

To get your creative juices pumping, here are more examples with potential impacts based on the examples already mentioned:

- a years-long friendship which morphs into the romantic after a trauma will not only have the change in relationship structure to deal with but also the switches in behaviour from the trauma survivor.
- for the characters who experience a bank robbery together, shared trauma can become a beneficial bonding experience, but it can also create trauma triggers upon seeing the other person.
- a character, who witnesses the post-trauma symptoms of their brother or sister, encounters a person who shared the trauma experience with their sibling, and they 'feel a spark' with the person. What a mess! Your character would need to deal with post-trauma effects from the sibling as well as the new person, and consider the power dynamics and ethics.

See how the different plot choices affect the way the post-trauma effects could impact the romantic relationships of the trauma survivor? These are the different aspects you will need to add into your plot and relationship arc. Some will be easier to write, and others will be more complex. The direction you move in depends on what you feel confident enough to write, your overall story idea, and your chosen trauma-themed subgenre requirements.

Questions and Exercises

1. Which romantic relationships will you show being impacted by your character/s post-trauma effects?
2. What stage is the romantic relationship? Will this make a difference to the romance?
3. What are the power and relationship dynamics? How will these change over the course of the story?
4. Will the relationship structure change? How? Why?
5. Will there be other changes to the romantic relationship? What will these be?

Chapter 13 – How Do Post-Trauma Effects Impact Non-Romantic Relationships?

As mentioned in the previous chapter, <u>all</u> relationships tend to be impacted post-trauma. Some of the non-romantic relationships you might want to think about trauma impacting in your novel include:

- family (immediate and extended)
- friends
- work colleagues
- acquaintances
- business partnerships

Potential Impact Areas

Like romantic relationships, non-romantic relationships can be impacted by anything that changes the dynamics of the relationship. For example, if your character was the 'life of the party' before the trauma and they have suddenly withdrawn into their shell, avoid people, and will not leave the house ... you can see how this could disrupt the lives of those who are used to the character being more lively. What about work colleagues? If your traumatised character was a workaholic, then stops showing up to work, how will their colleagues and family respond?

You can have some characters step up to support the survivor—try having someone unexpected rise to the occasion. Other characters will fail miserably. Surprisingly, the most typical reaction in 'real life' seems to be a neutral avoidance. Meaning: loved ones do not show they care, they will not offer support, and they will say/do nothing. Sometimes, this is because people 'don't know what to say/do', but other times it is done to avoid personal discomfort. Many trauma survivors lose friends, family, romantic relationships, businesses, and jobs because of this behaviour, so these are all viable plot pathways.

As per the romantic relationship impacts, have a think about the ways power dynamics, relationship dynamics, relationship structures, and other areas could be impacted by the changes in the trauma survivor. If you skipped that chapter, go back and read it now so you can apply that knowledge here.

Similarly to the stage of the romantic relationship, the level of closeness (and years of knowing) the traumatised character could change the way non-romantic relationships are impacted—and represented in your fiction. For instance, someone a character has known a week might react in a different way to the character's mother or a high school friend. Are there close non-romantic relationships that could grow an even stronger bond? Could the closeness be compromised by avoidant behaviour? Is there a new character who could support the trauma survivor, thereby increasing the level of closeness? Play with these dynamics and see what you can craft.

You might also want to include the trauma survivor's reactions to these changes, both from themselves and those around them. Does it make them feel worse, better, more numb, or more determined? How will their personal life look by the end of the book?

Questions and Exercises

1. Which non-intimate relationships will you show being impacted by your character/s post-trauma effects?
2. Will the level of closeness of the relationship matter?
3. What are the power and relationship dynamics? How will these change?
4. Will the relationship structure change? How? Why?
5. Will there be other changes to the non-romantic relationships? What will these be?
6. How will the trauma survivor react to all of these changes?

Chapter 14 – What is Trauma Recovery?

Please note: *The information in this chapter applies mostly to the post-trauma subgenres.*

From Trauma to Post-Trauma Recovery

How does a trauma survivor move from trauma to the post-trauma recovery stage? Figure 1 offers a visual summary of the most-accepted theoretical steps mapping the transition from trauma to post-trauma recovery. It does *not* consider every intricacy of trauma and its recovery process. Instead, think of Figure 1 as a form of the 'heroine or hero's journey', but for trauma. I reiterate at this point that trauma recovery is not a 'follow these exact steps to be healed forever' kind of journey. Trauma is more like a massive upward spiral: it never seems to end, sometimes it feels like you have gone back to the beginning, and other times you are sure you have been in the exact spot before. Avoid portraying your characters as 'healed' instead of on a continuing path to recovery.

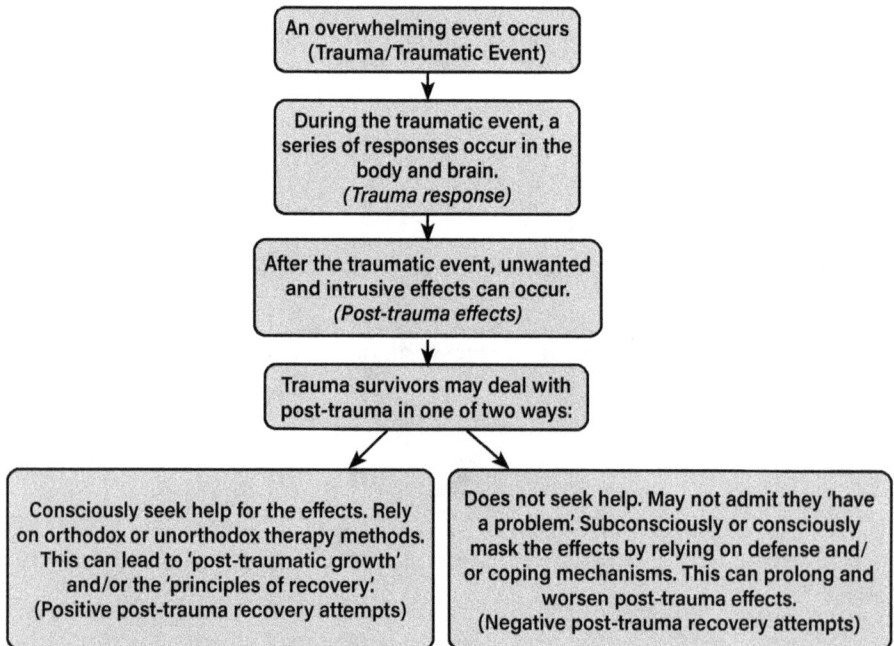

An overwhelming event occurs
(Trauma/Traumatic Event)

↓

During the traumatic event, a series of responses occur in the body and brain.
(*Trauma response*)

↓

After the traumatic event, unwanted and intrusive effects can occur.
(*Post-trauma effects*)

↓

Trauma survivors may deal with post-trauma in one of two ways:

↙ ↘

Consciously seek help for the effects. Rely on orthodox or unorthodox therapy methods. This can lead to 'post-traumatic growth' and/or the 'principles of recovery'.
(Positive post-trauma recovery attempts)

Does not seek help. May not admit they 'have a problem'. Subconsciously or consciously mask the effects by relying on defense and/or coping mechanisms. This can prolong and worsen post-trauma effects.
(Negative post-trauma recovery attempts)

Figure 1: Steps from trauma to post-trauma recovery
Source: Kindleysides 2024, p. 191

Figure 1 demonstrates how a traumatic event occurs (trauma), which causes a series of automatic responses (initial trauma responses), that can lead to intrusive and unwanted symptoms which interfere in a survivor's life (post-trauma effects and lingering trauma responses), and can lead to the survivor taking positive or negative steps towards dealing with the symptoms (post-trauma recovery attempts). This is the basic sequence you will show in your fiction, so ensure you read over Figure 1 several times to lock the concepts into your mind.

The previous chapters have guided you through establishing your character's traumatic experience, their initial trauma responses, and some possible post-trauma effects. Therefore, the next decision you will need to make is whether your character will choose to deal with their post-trauma effects in a positive or negative way. Of course, they can choose a negative approach at the start, but they **must** make a conscious, positive choice before the end of the book if you are writing in one of the post-trauma subgenres (since a conscious and positive recovery is one of the discerning features of the post-trauma subgenres). With that in mind, let us have a look at the multitude of trauma recovery therapies at your disposal.

Trauma Recovery Therapies

Trauma recovery therapies — which I refer to as the techniques, methods, and tools used in dealing with post-trauma effects — are far from a modern invention. It was only after World War 1, with the increasing appearance of severe post-trauma effects in returned soldiers, that psychologists realised there was a likely need for therapies to assist in trauma recovery. Along with this, as Figure 1 showed, trauma survivors often intuitively attempt recovery in positive or negative ways. Negative methods include the coping and defence mechanisms already discussed. My research showed that positive and conscious recovery attempts – in other words, when a survivor intentionally seeks out positive methods of assistance for trauma-related symptoms and behaviours — can be separated into two basic types (though I do not declare they are the only possible ones): orthodox therapy and unorthodox therapy.

Before continuing, a salient factor to bear in mind is that some therapeutic techniques work for some people, and *no* technique currently has a 100% success rate (otherwise, every psychologist would suggest its use and there would be no more debates in psychological or trauma theory). Further to this, a technique might work for an individual sometimes, and not at other times. Again, avoid showing any technique as a universal 'saving grace'. Following this advice will help you to limit ethical issues, misrepresentation traps, and deviations from research-backed trauma theory. In other words, it will help with writing authentic trauma elements.

Orthodox therapy includes all the traditional, psychological, psychoanalytical, and other 'talk therapies'; whereas unorthodox therapies are any therapeutic intervention which sits outside of the orthodox framework. The two distinct methods are neither wholly good nor bad (nor positive nor negative). Judge them on whether they help the trauma survivor (i.e. your character) or not. That being said, due to personal and professional experience, I confess my bias towards the unorthodox — which will become apparent as you read this chapter — so absorb the following information with that bias in mind.

Moreover, the ideas around accepted, orthodox treatments have changed. For instance, most psychologists and theorists view traditional psychoanalysis, as promoted by German psychologist and researcher Sigmund Freud, as having limited therapeutic value. As such, it is reasonable to assume the ideas around accepted orthodox therapies will continue to alter. Indeed, many of the methods currently viewed as unorthodox are gaining more attention and credibility: the unorthodox is becoming orthodox.

Despite this growing acceptance of the unorthodox, many psychologists and theorists still currently consider the following more orthodox therapies as suitable forms of therapeutic intervention:

- traditional psychology and psychotherapy
- Cognitive Behavioural Therapy (CBT)
- Acceptance and Commitment Therapy (ACT)
- exposure therapy

It would be reckless and inaccurate to claim these forms of therapy have not helped anybody and have no use in the positive trauma recovery process, in both the short and long-term. Therefore, even though there is a clear shift towards the unorthodox becoming more orthodox, these other more traditional methods can still currently be used in trauma-themed novels and align with accepted conventions. However, I flag here that this might not be the case in a decade or two, so if you want your novel to remain relevant for longer, you might want to consider shifting your plot towards the more unorthodox therapies.

Consider also that, according to Linda Grabbe and Elaine Miller-Karas 'body-based therapies may be more effective for trauma than currently used cognitive ("top-down") and exposure therapies'. The so-called top-down approach is what I refer to as 'orthodox therapy' and includes all traditional, psychological, psychoanalytical, and other 'talk therapies' — therapeutic approaches which require the client to talk about their challenges or issues. Commenting on the orthodox psychotherapies, Cathy Malchiodi ponders 'if there will come a time when mental health professionals will wonder why we were so intensely focused on talk as the cure for all that ails'. Therefore, these experts agree that there is a growing trend towards the more unorthodox therapies when it comes to trauma recovery.

As is probably obvious by now, I have also reached this conclusion. My lived experience traversing the psychological therapy path further showcases this increasing switch towards the unorthodox. Body-based therapies make up part of the suite of the increasingly accepted unorthodox therapies. These largely (though not entirely) 'bottom-up' therapies require the use of the body to regulate brain responses, thus (theoretically) intervening in trauma response and short-circuiting unpleasant effects. Therefore, activities such as yoga, dance, grounding exercises, meditation, relaxation exercises, and 'body scans' fall into this category.

To clarify: orthodox therapy refers to any interventions which maintain a top-down (i.e. using the brain to assist in regulating trauma responses in the body) or talk-based approach, such as traditional psychotherapy, all talking-based therapies, and exposure therapies. In contrast, the term unorthodox therapy refers to any interventions which maintain a bottom-up — namely, using the body to aid in regulating trauma responses in the BBANS, thereby limiting and/or lowering post-trauma effects — or non-verbal approach, such as body-movement exercises, 'expressive arts' (such as writing), and creativity. You might choose one or more of these for your characters to experiment with. Alternatively, you can choose a more orthodox approach with your character undergoing psychotherapy or traditional counselling. If you really want to cover your bases or experiment, you could even have your character undergoing a combination of orthodox *and* unorthodox therapies. You are the best person to know which type of therapy will help your character the most.

Resilience and Post-Traumatic Growth

What do I mean by 'help'? I mean, does the therapy promote resilience/post-traumatic growth — which is the positive change that can come after a traumatic experience — and the so-called 'principles of recovery' (as posited by researcher Marie Crowe). In other words, does the therapy support a positive 'path to recovery' or 'process of recovery'? This should be the target outcome regardless of the therapy type employed. Which leads to the problem of a particular process to follow on the path to recovery. Although a more detailed overview of this occurs in an upcoming chapter, to start the conversation around a possible path to recovery that your characters can follow, two correlated concepts, mentioned above, need to be overviewed as they pertain to the recovery process: resilience and post-traumatic growth (PTG).

Resilience, originally posited by Roger Luckhurst, is 'positive adaptation within the context of significant adversity'. To simplify this concept, Thompson states that 'resilience is the ability to bounce back from adversity, trauma, or stress'. In comparison, Lawrence G Calhoun and Richard G Tedeschi describe post-traumatic growth as a long-revered idea that positive change can come from a traumatic experience. Bond and Craps note that PTG is 'closely related to resilience' and is associated with positive 'changes in the domains of self-perception, interpersonal relationships, and life philosophy'. Drawing on the opinions of these theorists, I argue that positive change is the ideal outcome for a trauma survivor through post-trauma recovery attempts.

Another pertinent concept to overview at this point is the 'window of tolerance' — this concept corresponds with what is known as the 'optimal zone of arousal'. According to renowned clinical psychiatrist Dan Siegel, the window of tolerance refers to the (emotional, psychological, mental, etc.) boundaries/

limits of our BBANS to remain in a state of balance. When a trauma survivor is hyperaroused, hypoaroused, or otherwise experiencing a post-trauma effect, they are outside of their window of tolerance. The goal of therapy, then, is to widen the window of tolerance, limit the potential for moving outside of the window, and strengthen the window's boundaries. The trauma therapy techniques listed in the next chapter can offer short-term, quick opportunities for trauma survivors to move back into the window, whereas an individualised positive recovery process can offer long-term opportunities for widening the window and strengthening its boundaries. As an aside, I align the concept of the window of tolerance with the terms 'regulated versus dysregulated', with regulated being inside the window of tolerance (within the optimal zone of arousal) and dysregulated being outside the window (outside the optimal zone of arousal).

Questions and Exercises

The questions and exercises listed below will ask you to think about how your characters will traverse the trauma to post-trauma recovery journey. Again, these exercises will only be fully relevant to those looking to write transitional post-trauma (transitional subgenres can include this as one of two feature options) and post-trauma subgenres. In the case of those intending to write in the trauma subgenre, you may only need to complete the first exercise. You also might need to come back to these exercises after reading other chapters of this book, since your ideas might evolve or change. To be safe, bookmark this page now.

Have a think about how your character's trauma recovery journey is going to progress. Then consider these questions:

- will they make a conscious choice to seek out therapy?
- will someone else force them into therapy?
- will they try to self-medicate with drugs and/or alcohol first?
- will they try to engage in their own form of positive therapy?
- who/what will help them along the way?
- who/what will hinder them along the way?
- how will they finally start their conscious and positive recovery journey?

Chapter 15 – How to Represent a Character Undergoing Therapy on Their Recovery Journey: The Therapy Sessions

Representing a character's journey in therapy is probably going to be the hardest part of your writing. Not only might you need to showcase a therapy session, but you may also need to show specific techniques which are designed to help your character. What you portray will mostly depend on personal choice, so long as some sort of recovery is shown (if you are writing the post-trauma subgenres). It can be tricky, from both a personal and moral perspective, but it can be achieved if you break it down into the therapy sessions and the specific 'technique timeframes'. This chapter deals with the former topic and subsequent chapters will look at the technique timeframes.

Below is an overview of the basic skills used in a typical counselling/ psychology therapy session. Regardless of whether your client character decides on orthodox or unorthodox therapy, they will most likely have to receive said therapy during a formal session of some kind. You can choose to depict some, all, one, or none of these sessions – according to the requirements of your chosen subgenre. Your therapist/counsellor/psychologist/mental health care character can employ some or all of the following skills in the therapy sessions your character attends. In the professional jargon, the skills are known as 'micro skills'.

What are Micro Skills?

Micro skills are the foundational tools used by professional counsellors and therapists to elicit feelings of safety, acceptance, and being understood in the client. They are also used to gather details about the client's 'story' to assist in choosing the most applicable therapy techniques for the recovery journey. For further information on counselling and counselling skills, you might like to check out Ivey, Ivey, and Zalaquett's informative book — see the *Recommended Reading and References*. Some of the basic micro skills are:

1. Reflecting feelings

- when the character says something which highlights a particular feeling, get the therapist to reflect this back to them.
- examples: 'You're saying the bank robbery made you feel scared for your life?' or 'It sounds like you might have been afraid you were going to die during the bank robbery?'

2. Encouraging

- these are simple one- or two-word phrases used to encourage the character to continue and/or divulge more information.
- examples: 'I see', 'okay', 'go on', 'what else?', 'I'm listening', and 'then what?'
- they can also be simple gestures like a head nod or smile, and sounds/verbals like 'mm-hmm' and 'uh-huh'. Open body language — when the arms and legs do not cross over each other but remain open and inviting — is another form of encouraging. Anything that encourages the character to continue can be considered a use of the encouraging micro skill.

3. Paraphrasing

- this is an overview of what the character has said. It typically involves the employment of a so-called 'sentence stem'.
- examples: 'I'm hearing you say ...', 'It sounds to me like ...', and 'It's as if ...'. After paraphrasing what the character said, the therapist ends with a check in, such as 'is that right?' or 'am I understanding that/you correctly?'. For instance, you could have the therapist say to the traumatised character, 'It seems like you felt scared for your life during the bank robbery, is that correct?' I recommend using this micro skill sparingly in your fiction because it can become boring to re-read the same information. Even so, it could also be used to great effect as a form of repetition.

4. Summarising

- a longer version of paraphrasing. Usually, summarising would take place at the end or beginning of a session. At the beginning, the therapist would go over what the character had expressed in the previous session.

- Examples: 'Last week, we talked about ...'. At the end of the session, the therapist would summarise the entire session. For instance, 'Today, we talked about ...'. Notice the use of 'we' in both of the example sentences provided? Using 'we' instead of 'you' is another technique used by mental health professionals since 'we' promotes an aura of collaboration, cooperation, and sharing. Again, limit the representation of this micro skill in your fiction for the same reasons discussed under paraphrasing.

5. Restating

- The therapist repeats, word-for-word, exactly what the traumatised character said. This develops trust and shows the character they are being heard, understood, and listened to. For the same reasons as paraphrasing and summarising, limit the use of restating in your fiction.
- Example: 'Mm-hmm. It was soooo scary being in the bank robbery' (note the use of an encourager along with repetition of the same inflections/accents used by the character: 'soooo').

6. Asking questions (the right ones)

- In counselling and psychotherapy, there is a strategic quality to questions. The therapist cannot keep bombarding the traumatised character with questions (or else it can come across as an interrogation). Instead, the questions have to lead to specific goals and outcomes. These goals and outcomes are commonly a) uncovering the story/reason for seeking help, b) discovering unwanted symptoms and behaviours, c) checking in on progress, and d) deciding which therapeutic interventions would work best.
- Examples for a) include: 'What is it that has brought you to see me today?', 'What happened next?', and 'Did anything else happen?'
- An example of b) is: 'You said before that you sometimes have unwanted images of the bank robbery come into your head. Could you tell me more about that?' — this is also a type of paraphrasing, showing how your therapist can incorporate one or more of the micro skills together.
- Example for c): you could have the therapist ask, 'How did you go with the journalling exercise we set for last week?' (note the use of 'we').

- Examples for option d) include: 'What artistic activities do you like?' (to see if art therapy would be an ideal choice), 'How do you feel when you talk about what happened to you?' (to check if talk therapy helps or makes them feel worse), and 'Have you ever tried meditation?' (to see if mindfulness could be used).

7. Empathy

- This micro skill involves choosing strategic moments to express empathy for what the client has gone through.
- Example: in response to the character sharing that they had felt afraid during a bank robbery, the therapist could say, 'That sounds scary', 'I can understand why you felt scared', or 'That must have been terrifying for you'. More general empathetic phrases can also be used: 'That sounds tough', 'I understand', or 'That must have felt awful'.

Again, this is a basic, beginner-level list of micro skills. There are more advanced micro skills that a therapist can use. If you are interested in learning more, please feel free to add a note in your notebook to research micro skills during the questions and exercises section at the end of this chapter. In the meantime, the above 7 micro skills can be immediately implemented into your therapist-character interactions. Table 10 contains a list of the 7 basic micro skills with their associated definitions for easy reference.

Micro Skill	Definition
Reflecting feelings	The therapist reflecting the character's feelings back to them
Encouraging	Simple one- or two-word phrases used to encourage the character to continue and/or divulge more information
Paraphrasing	An overview of what the character has said using sentence stems
Summarising	A longer version of paraphrasing, often employed at the beginning and end of a session

Asking questions	Strategic questions to: uncover the reason for seeking help, discover unwanted symptoms, check progress, and decide on a therapeutic intervention
Empathy	Choosing strategic moments to express empathy for what the client has gone through

Table 10: The Seven Basic Micro Skills
Source: Author

While it is great to know what the micro skills are, understanding where/ when to apply them in a counselling session takes another skill. Below, I have provided an introductory therapy session template for you to adapt. Note: this is for guidance only. There are many variables which affect how a session goes. Also, the introductory session will differ from follow up sessions in subtle ways. For instance, the therapist is not going to need to ask the traumatised character what brought them to the session, since this information would have been obtained in the first session (as you will soon see).

An Introductory Therapy Session Template

The first therapy session between a client character and the therapist character can be the hardest to write. That is why I am providing this template. The therapist character needs to build rapport and trust to allow the client character to open up ... and the therapist must <u>also</u> build rapport with your *reader*. If the reader dislikes/distrusts the therapist, or thinks they are not being sympathetic, you might lose readers or impact how well the manuscript is received. Furthermore, if the character does not trust the therapist, this can cause conflict (and is a plot point to consider. I had Neoma in *The Love Healer* go through several therapists before landing on Emerson). Therefore, the introductory therapy session is a crucial scene. To craft it with authenticity, accuracy, and sensitivity:

1. Build rapport between the traumatised character and therapist (and reader and therapist)

- do this by having the therapist be warm and welcoming from the first moment. Have the therapist smile and say something inviting like, 'Please come in and sit wherever you find comfortable'. Throughout the scene, the therapist, specifically as it pertains to trauma, and depending on the precise circumstances of the traumatic event, could also use vast amounts of open body language, avoid turning their back on the client, limit quick or jerky movements, give the client plenty of physical space, and/or keep their hands visible at all times.

2. Use micro skills to flesh out the character's story

- once the character has chosen a seat, the therapist should take theirs then use an introductory question, such as, 'What is it that has brought you here to see me today?' When the answer comes, the therapist can keep using micro skills to flesh out the story.

3. (Optional/add to later sessions) Use micro skills to flesh out any troubling symptoms and behaviours

- typically, once the character starts their story, they will mention, sometimes in an off-the-cuff way some symptoms and behaviours that are worrying them.

4. Goals.

- get the therapist to ask the character what they want to achieve in therapy. They can ask straight out like that (i.e., 'what do you want to achieve in therapy') or in a more subtle way, such as 'What do you hope to achieve by coming here?'

5. Summarise and end the session

- summarise what has happened in the session so far, end the session, and arrange a subsequent visit.

As the sessions progress, the therapist will suggest different therapeutic techniques to assist the character in their recovery process. Sometimes, this step can occur in the first session. This depends on the way you write it, your plot, your characters, and your level of confidence in writing the scenes. It will also depend on whether you are using orthodox or unorthodox therapies, and whether your traumatised character is getting professional help (individual, group, and/ or family therapy) or going it alone via reading books, going to workshops, or attending classes. Options for this step are discussed in the following chapters (note: sometimes, talking about their story **is** the recovery process for the traumatised character. Think Freud and psychoanalysis. This is the essence of traditional 'talk therapy'. Write it down in your notebook now if this is a topic you would like to explore in more detail.

Example Therapy Session Based on the Introductory Therapy Session Template

The following scene includes examples of all the steps and listed micro skills— and others—detailed in bold in brackets:

I opened the door and saw a man, who I assumed to be my new client, Sieg, standing before me. His gaze darted from my face to beside and around me, then back to my face; his hands were clasped together in a tight grip in front of his pelvis. I smiled, hoping to calm his obvious anxiety (start of step 1).

Then, I said, 'You must be Sieg. It's a pleasure to meet you. Please come in.'

He gave me a suspicious glance, so I smiled again and stood aside, giving him plenty of room to enter my office (providing physical space). After a moment of hesitation, he stepped into the room.

I said, 'Feel free to sit wherever you like.'

As he glanced around my office, I closed the door in as slow and as quiet a manner as I could, then walked with a steady pace towards my chair (**limiting jerky and quick movements**). He had chosen a seat far from mine, in the opposite corner of the room, showing he did not quite trust me yet. Or maybe he didn't want to be here. Maybe both?

Using a slow movement (**limiting jerky and quick movements**), I swivelled my chair in his direction (**open body language and avoiding having their back to the character**). His gaze searched the room. For a subconscious feeling of safety?

To help put him at ease, I said, 'I'm so glad you could come, Sieg. Would you like to tell me what it is you came to see me about?' (**introductory question and start of step 2**)

He hesitated, then, in an almost-whisper said, 'Uh, there was a bank robbery'.

'I see. There was a bank robbery.' (**encouraging and restating**)

'Yes.'

'Is it okay if you tell me more about that?' (**question. Note: asking 'is it okay if ...' is a good technique to use with resistant characters since it offers choice**)

He nodded, but didn't say anything. I could see his still-clasped hands turning white.

'It's okay. Take your time.' (**encouraging**)

He threw me an assessing look-over, then said, 'I was one of the hostages.'

'Oh, wow. That must have been a tough experience, Sieg.' (**encouraging and empathy. Also, using the character name can help build rapport when used at strategic moments**)

'It was.'

'Can I ask what the toughest part about it was?' (**question and offering choice**)

- 'Probably how scared I felt.'
- 'Mm-hmm. It felt scary being in a bank robbery.' (**encouraging and reflection of feelings**)
- 'Yes.'
- 'I can understand why it was scary.' (**empathy**)
- 'Thank you ...'
- He said the words softly, almost as is they hadn't been said at all, and seemed to drift off at the end. There was something going on here.
- 'I get the feeling something is happening for you around feeling scared. Is that accurate?' (**question and 'probing' — questions used to help clients explore their thoughts, feelings, and experiences. It encourages them to expand, clarify, uncover more details, gain insights, and address hidden/avoidant information**)
- He flinched. I was right. He was avoiding something, and was not ready to talk about it yet. I had to tread lightly.
  - 'We don't have to go into that today. How about you tell me what you

want me to know about the bank robbery instead, is that okay?' (**question and offering choice**)

- He sucked in a breath and rubbed his hands together in a nervous gesture. 'Well, it's, actually, I've been having problems sleeping.'
    - 'You've been having problems sleeping since the bank robbery?' (**paraphrasing and start of optional step 3**)
    - 'Yes.'
    - 'What specifically has been happening with your sleep?' (**question**)
    - He sighed. 'It's been terrible. Every time I close my eyes, I remember it.'
    - 'You dream about the bank robbery?' (**question. This is also the use of another micro skill called 'clarification', in which a question is asked to clarify details**)
    - 'Yes.'
    - 'I see. That can't be easy for you.' (**encouraging and empathy**)
    - 'It's not.'
    - 'I'm sure. Okay, so far, you've told me you were in a scary bank robbery and you have been having problems sleeping. Is that right?' (**empathy, summarising, and clarification**)
    - 'Yes.'
    - 'In that case, can I ask what you hope to achieve in our sessions together?' (**offering choice, use of we/our to encourage rapport, and start of step 4**)
- He looked up at the ceiling, as if the heavens would give him the answer. 'I just want to be able to ... I don't know ...' He sighed and looked at me.
- 'That's fine. We don't have to have all the answers yet. We can work on that together if you like.' (**encouraging, use of we, and offering choice**)
- He nodded. 'I'd like that.' (**rapport and trust building**)
- I smiled. 'Wonderful. How about I schedule you in for the same time next week and we can talk about it more then?' (**choice and start of step 5**)
- He exhaled in a clear sign of relief then moved his clasped hands to his lap, relaxing a little. 'That sounds great.'
    - 'Great. Thank you so much for coming in today, Sieg. How about I walk out with you?' (**mild restating — 'great' — and use of name**)

As you can see, you can play around with some of the elements. In the provided example, you will notice I used other micro skills and altered some of the steps, such as having the summarising occur in step 3 rather than step 5. The example also showed how much information you can give to readers in such a short sequence. For example, although the reader does not know Sieg's full experience of the bank robbery, they have been introduced to a fragment of the story. The reader can also see that the trauma has affected him to the extent that he is on edge, hyperalert, avoidant, and having trouble sleeping (a mixture of hyperaroused and hypoaroused symptoms). You can choose to have the full traumatic experience revealed primarily through therapy sessions such as the example given, or you can use a variety of plotting methods already discussed, such as dream sequences and news stories.

Questions and Exercises

Feel free to skip these exercises if you do not plan on including post-trauma recovery elements in your novel

1. Do you think your character will do best with orthodox, unorthodox, or a combination of both therapies? (More specific techniques are detailed in upcoming chapters)
2. What specific type of therapy will it be? (For instance, will your character receive talk-therapy only? Will they attend a group-based trauma-informed dance class? See an unorthodox art-based therapist? Start a writing or journalling practice based on a trauma-writing book they have been given?).
3. How many therapy sessions will you portray? (One session? Two? Several? All? None?)
4. Will you use the introductory session template for inspiration?
5. What micro skills will you use?
6. Is there anything else you need to note at this time?

Chapter 16 – An Overview of the Technique Timeframes

Alongside the therapy sessions, your traumatised characters will need to be provided with tools and techniques to help them move forward in their trauma recovery journeys. To achieve this, the therapist character (or book/workshop/YouTube videos/class instructions, if your traumatised character is going solo) will need to suggest methods for the traumatised character to try. Although techniques abound, some have been found to work better when applied during different timeframes.

What are technique timeframes?

I coined this term to refer to the three basic timeframes within which certain trauma recovery techniques are best utilised. The three technique timeframes are: immediate (aimed at preventing post-trauma effects as soon as safely possible after the trauma), short-term/first-aid (to deal with triggered post-trauma effects whenever they occur), and a long-term 'path to recovery' or 'process of recovery'. The latter is designed to lessen the impact of effects, expand the window of tolerance/optimal zone of arousal/regulated levels, and limit potential triggers for the traumatised character in the long-term. Here is an overview of each technique timeframe before we dive into each one in more detail in the proceeding chapters.

Immediate Techniques

I have offered a glimpse at a couple of immediate post-trauma recovery techniques which can be utilised by your characters as soon as is safely possible after their traumatic experience, namely, shaking, rocking, swaying, general movement, and sleep, so I will not repeat that information here. Remember, minimal research has been carried out on immediate interventions. Even so, using the aforementioned techniques in your fiction will not go against any current research. Indeed, trauma specialist Dr Peter Levine has spoken of his own anecdotal experience with the immediate methods. He was hit by a car and started shaking/shivering (<u>not</u>

108

convulsing/fitting) involuntarily in the ambulance on the way to the hospital. When a nurse offered him medication to halt the shaking, he declined, informing her that he believed it was his body's natural attempt at preventing a long-term post-trauma response. He says he has had no PTSD or other negative, lingering post-trauma symptoms from the event. Interesting stuff, right? Another proviso: ensure your character can safely carry out these techniques. Do not get them to try and shake or rock if they are in traction!

Short-Term/First-Aid Techniques

The next chapter details multiple orthodox and unorthodox techniques (backed by research) that your traumatised characters can use to aid them when triggered in the short-term. They are good optimal zone of arousal/window of tolerance/regulating techniques. Short-term techniques can also be considered first-aid techniques in that they can be the first line of treatment for triggered characters.

Long-Term Techniques

Several upcoming chapters feature details of the three-step positive recovery process (3SPRP) I devised during my PhD research. The 3SPRP deals with a longer-term technique/intervention for trauma survivors. It is essential to portray a long-term recovery process for at least one traumatised character in the post-trauma subgenres.

When to Depict the Techniques

You can depict these techniques during the character's therapy sessions (have the therapist teach them), and also have the traumatised character use them outside of the therapeutic environment. This is what I had Neoma do in *The Love Healer*. In the early post-trauma period, you might even have therapists, hospital workers, paramedics, and/or friends suggest or teach the survivor some of the techniques.

Once again, if you wish to dive deeper and/or present your character/s undergoing a specific recovery therapy/technique/tool/method not addressed in this guide (remember, there is **a lot** of possibility in this field and I cannot cover everything in one book), you will need to rely on your research skills. As such, if there is a particular therapy you want to incorporate, and the details are not found in this book, you might want to follow these steps:

1. Choose the therapy you would like to explore
2. Buy books/courses on those specific therapies
3. Learn the fundamentals
4. Use your new knowledge to represent the therapy in your story (rely on the 'facts')
5. Ensure you follow the suggestions for limiting potential triggers and victim blaming

Whichever recovery techniques you choose to represent, the goal is the same: showing how the traumatised character develops new ideas of themselves and their trauma experience, easing unwanted and intrusive post-trauma symptoms and behaviours, expanding regulated periods, and developing positive trigger management skills (short-term/first-aid techniques). If you have the character choosing to 'go it alone', you would show them engaging in their chosen recovery therapy techniques, then represent the slow, positive changes that occur.

Questions and Exercises

1. Will you represent immediate, short-term, and/or long-term recovery techniques in your book? (note: if you are writing in the post-trauma subgenres, you will <u>need</u> to show some kind of recovery process)
2. Will your character perform any immediate techniques, such as shaking exercises, rocking, movement, or deep sleep (REM)?
3. When will you depict these techniques in your story?
4. If you are carrying out more research, have you followed the suggested steps? If not, do that now.

Chapter 17 – Short-Term Techniques for Post-Trauma Effects in Your Characters, Part 1

Triggered post-trauma effects, and those caused by the lingering mode, can be addressed in a targeted manner at the time the effect is occurring, by engaging in specific techniques. For instance, if a 'fright' response is noted, then, being associated with a state of hypoarousal (as well as hyperarousal; fright straddles the fence), hypoarousal-directed techniques can be used to assist the trauma survivor.

I divide the upcoming techniques into those for hyperaroused, hypoaroused, and 'both' states. I advocate for this division not because I believe the other ways are wrong or unhelpful, but because, in a post-trauma state, the survivor is (usually) not thinking, 'Is this a freeze response or fade response? What am I supposed to do for that again?'. Keeping with authentic and accurate representation of trauma, then, you need to consider this with your characters. By dividing the following techniques more simply into hyperaroused, hypoaroused, and both categories, it is easier to manage, especially if traumatised characters are guided through their main responses by a qualified therapist and taught the corresponding techniques. As the term 'both' indicates, there are techniques I feel can work for everyone—regardless of their state. Therefore, if you are really unsure as to what techniques to use for your characters, stick to the ones marked 'both'. These techniques are best for use when the individual is too dysregulated to think about which type of arousal they are experiencing, or when they do not know. Or, they have been found to work for many people.

A reminder here that hyperaroused states are identifiable by physiological adaptations which align with the lingering trauma responses of:

- Fright
- Flood
- Freeze
- Flight
- Fight
- Fawn
- Fade

Hypoaroused states are identifiable by physiological adaptations which align with the lingering trauma responses of:

- Fright
- Faint
- Flag

To make the information on these short-term and first-aid recovery techniques easier to grasp, I have divided them into three chapters: one for the hyperaroused (this chapter) post-trauma effects, one for the hypoaroused, and one for both. After each prescribed technique to come, I have included in brackets whether the technique is currently associated with unorthodox, orthodox, or both therapies. This may help you when picking something for your character, to align with the therapy you chose in the previous chapters.

Please check with a doctor and/or mental health practitioner if you wish to engage in any of the following activities yourself, since this book is designed primarily for use in crafting trauma in *fiction*. Dealing with trauma and its impact in real-life is a different type of story, which often requires professional assistance.

Techniques for Hypervigilance/Hyperarousal Triggered Effects

The activities under this subheading are designed to release extra energy, slow the brain down, and help the BBANS relax into a feeling of safety. Doing this promotes a healthy rebalancing of safety and danger mechanisms and increases the window of tolerance. You will notice the listed techniques are on a spectrum from fairly active to somewhat passive. This is because different activities have been found to help different people. Much like real humans, story characters are unique, so one technique will not necessarily work on every character. The following are those techniques which many survivors in a hyperaroused state have found helpful, and are adapted from a range of therapeutic models and therapists (I do not claim *all* of them as my original ideas and acknowledge the work of the theorists who came before me). Some of these techniques are well-established in popular culture, but have been given a therapeutic, research-backed twist. I have also adapted, slightly altered, and/or combined other techniques according to the research. Use your intuition, along with the knowledge of your character (and their specific trauma), when deciding whether to represent any of the following techniques in your manuscript. You could also choose to rely solely on the specific therapy you chose to research as part of the exercises in the last chapter.

Several exercises you can use for your characters are:

1. Engaging the senses (both)

There is an exercise known as the 5-4-3-2-1 Grounding Exercise. This involves having your character name (aloud) five things they can see, four things they can touch/feel, three things they can hear, two things they can smell, and one thing they can taste.

1A. The more active version of the above technique is what I call 'Wake up the Senses' (both)

For this technique, have the character smell something pungent, like an onion, garlic, or black pepper. Then, have them taste something bitter or acidic, like a lemon, apple cider vinegar, or unsweetened black coffee. Next, get them to touch something rough or prickly (but not sharp — you do not want your character hurting themselves) like a pineapple skin, sandpaper, or emery board. The character should then listen to something, such as their favourite music. Finally, have the character look at something unusual (but not something scary or disturbing). It can be pictures of abstract art in a coffee table art book in the therapy office or visual puzzles.

Another dimension you might want to add to the 1 and 1A exercises is having a character ask the traumatised character if any of the experiences made them *feel* something. The traumatised character can note the answers in a journal or notebook if they are resistant to talking about it aloud. The aim of these exercises is to cut into the emotional response and encourage the pre-frontal cortex into taking over through focused thinking.

2. Exercise, especially cardio or aerobic activities which get the heart racing (both). This can be a great choice for characters who are athletic (but not if they have pre-existing health conditions that would rule this out. Remember to use the technique/s that would work best for the *character*). Some examples include:

- running
- power walking
- aerobics class
- swimming laps
- energetic dancing

2A. Star jumps/Jumping jacks (unorthodox)

Have the character perform for three sets of five–ten, or enough to cause panting/puffing. Another great option for the more athletically-inclined character because it can boost energy levels and 'wake up' the body.

3. ASMR, white noise, or repetitive 'shh' sound recordings (unorthodox)

ASMR refers to a type of, usually, audiovisual media which is designed to evoke what is known as an 'autonomous sensory meridian response' (hence, ASMR) — sometimes referred to as the 'tingles' or pleasant shivers. These types of sounds can create a feeling of calm, nurturance, and soothing to an overagitated BBANS. They might also be especially beneficial for those characters who lacked positive mothering experiences.

4. Weight lifting (unorthodox)

The character does not need to lift ultra-heavy weights, but they do need to be heavy enough to make the character aware of the weight. Again, this a good choice for characters who are athletic, or those wanting to be physically stronger to provide a psychological safety boost.

5. Chanting (unorthodox)

Any positive and repetitive sound, phrase, or word can be used, including the stereotypical 'Aum'. Other choices include a soothing 'shhh' or 'I am safe in this moment'.

6. Cognitive reframing/cognitive restructuring (orthodox)

Cognitive reframing (aka cognitive restructuring) is when a negative or unhelpful thought, idea, emotion, or feeling is identified then consciously replaced (i.e., 'reframed') in a positive and helpful way. It is best to have a therapist guide the character through this technique since it can be difficult for the character to do it themselves when they are hyperaroused. Get the therapist to ask the character to identify any negative thoughts, ideas, emotions, and/or feelings they are having around the trauma, such as, 'It was my fault'. The therapist could also ask a reframing question, such as, 'What is a different way to look at this situation?' or 'If this happened to a loved one, how would you tell them to look at this situation?' Have the therapist lead the character to a more positive viewpoint. Cognitive reframing techniques can also form part of a long-term recovery process.

7. Mindful slow breathing (both)
- since breath rate increases in hyperaroused states, focusing on slow (as opposed to 'deep') breathing — as advanced by breathing expert, James Nestor — can assist in bringing the PNS back in charge. There are many variations of slow breathing. The 'mindful slow breathing' technique, also known as '4-2-5-2 breathing', detailed in my PhD thesis is what I recommend. This is how to do it:
- inhale slowly to a count of four
- hold breath for a count of two
- breathe out slowly to a count of five
- finish by holding breath for another count of two
- repeat as many times as needed or until a feeling of calm is reached.

The mindful slow breathing technique can also be incorporated into a longer recovery process.

8. Progressive muscle relaxation (orthodox)

This is to help the character notice signs of tension before they arise. Again, it can form part of a longer recovery process. There are a variety of muscle relaxation exercises. Here is one I recommend:
- start at the legs.
- tense the calf muscles as you breathe in.
- relax the calf muscles as you breathe out (slower than you breathed in) and repeat aloud, 'relax'.

- progressively move up the body as you tense each successive muscle group and include the associated breathing.
- stop at the shoulders.

Obviously, this is only a snapshot of available techniques your character can employ. Did you find anything else in your research? Has the list given you any ideas of therapies or techniques to research? Do any of these appeal to your character? Write the answers to these questions in your notebook so you can explore them alongside the below questions and exercises.

Matching Character Preferences to Techniques

Modern therapy guidelines include considering client preferences when choosing potential therapeutic techniques. Thus, to remain accurate and authentic on your trauma-informed writer journey, the techniques can be matched in accordance with your character's preferences — this is where knowing your character will help you. I have alluded to some of these throughout the above techniques, for instance, review the techniques where I mentioned they are good choices for athletic characters. Some other examples are:

- swimming for swimming champion characters (unless they are recovering from a near-drowning, of course)
- chanting for more new-age or spiritual characters
- cognitive reframing for those characters who are analytical

You might also want to think about the type of physical exercise your character would enjoy. Or, sounds they would find soothing. Or, smells/sights/sounds/sensations/tastes that would help to jolt them awake in a 5-4-3-2-1 exercise. Using Sieg as an example, perhaps he was a champion runner in his youth, so this could be added to his therapy. Maybe, somewhat ironically, he also finds ASMR sounds of people running money through a cash counting machine soothing? This could be included too. What interesting, unique, or unusual match can you come up with for your character?

Questions and Exercises

If you have chosen a mostly hyperaroused character, what are some of the techniques described in this chapter that you might like to incorporate in your character therapy sessions and plot? Think about:

- your own interests
- the interests of your traumatised character (match their preferences)
- what you think you could portray
- whether it seems like a logical and intuitive recovery choice for the character, plot, and trauma arc
- do you need to carry out more research on your chosen recovery interventions?

Chapter 18 – Short-Term Techniques for Post-Trauma Effects in Your Characters, Part 2

These hypovigilance-/hypoaroused-centred activities are designed to wake up or shock (in a good way) the BBANS and slowly shake it out of its low arousal/energy state. The techniques also allow for a healthy, rebalanced safety and danger mechanism reforming in the BBANS.

Techniques for Hypovigilance/Hypoarousal Triggered Effects

As per the hyperaroused techniques, the hypoaroused suggestions range from passive to more active and your knowledge of your character should be used when deciding which, if any, of the following techniques you might represent in your story. Again, they are adapted from a range of therapeutic models and therapists, and I do not necessarily claim ownership or creation of *all* of the ideas. Brackets are, likewise, used to show whether the technique is considered orthodox, unorthodox, or both. Once again, check with a doctor and/or mental health practitioner if you wish to engage in any of the following activities yourself. The information to come is for *fictional* traumatised characters. Some of the suggested techniques for your traumatised characters are:

1. Gentle exercise (both)

    Gentle exercise can stimulate the SNS, pulling the body out of a PNS slump. Consider:

    - walking/Strolling (especially in nature)
    - stretching
    - pilates
    - yoga

2. Reading/bibliotherapy (unorthodox)

    Bibliotherapy is the therapeutic use of reading. Have the character choose a favourite genre and/or favourite book to read. It is best to avoid trauma triggering themes during a triggered state. Alternatively, the therapist can suggest books for the character (both fiction and non-fiction) to read. You might even have the character visit a bibliotherapist for what is known as a 'book prescription' — a book suggested by a bibliotherapist to assist in therapeutic recovery. Bibliotherapy can be an excellent choice when a character is on the ultra-low arousal end of the spectrum and nothing else can shake them into their optimum zone of arousal/window of tolerance/regulated state. This is because reading a favourite book/genre requires little physical effort but stimulates the brain and nervous system.

3. Writing/scriptotherapy (unorthodox)

Scriptotherapy is the therapeutic use of writing. For instance:

- journalling
- automatic writing
- astream of consciousness
- writing prompts

The character might also join a scriptotherapy writing group. Like bibliotherapy, a scriptotherapist can 'prescribe' specific writing activities for specific conditions to assist in the process of recovery. This technique might be a fantastic choice for those characters at a slightly higher low-level of arousal than the reading option requires.

4. Drawing, doodling, painting, or sketching, especially in nature (unorthodox)

'Art therapy' — a term denoting art used in a therapeutic way — is a wonderful therapeutic choice to represent if you wish to incorporate a quirky or interesting element into the story. Also good for the more artistic characters.

5. Nature therapy/green therapy (unorthodox)

These terms refer to therapy which incorporates nature. This can have wonderful benefits on the nervous system. Thus, combining it with other techniques can work well for those triggered into a hypoaroused post-trauma state. Have your characters go for walks in nature, spend time outside, or collect unusual rocks.

6. Slow or swaying/rocking types of dancing (unorthodox)

The reasons for this should be obvious from the information provided on the benefits of these types of movements in the immediate aftermath of trauma. There is some evidence to show they also have a positive effect when continued throughout the recovery process. Slow dancing, theoretically, works for the same PNS activating reasons as gentle exercise. Some choices include:

- slow waltz
- slow cha cha
- slow flamenco
- belly-dance

Alternatively, you can have characters sway, rock, and/or roll their hips (more on this option soon).

7. Dead hangs, dead hang swings, and standing dead hangs (unorthodox)

These are exercises I have found personally useful, so I am sharing them here. They can all stimulate the SNS, especially the longer they continue. Chin-up bars, monkey bars, or a sturdy door frame can be used to carry out these techniques. Dead hangs involve using your arms to grip onto a bar and dangling for a set amount of time. Dead hang swings incorporate a basic dead hang technique, with gentle swinging added in. For standing dead hangs swings, get your character to keep their feet on the floor (as strength and tolerance increases, have the character aim to be on their tiptoes), then start a soft swinging motion. The character should swing or sway any way that feels nice, for as long as it feels good. The long-term recovery process can include any of these dead hang variations.

8. Swinging (unorthodox)

Another activity which has helped me immensely, and can also be incorporated into the longer plan for recovery, is swinging. This works for the same reasons swaying/rocking works. I also think there is a subconscious connection to being rocked as a baby, which brings comfort to some people. Although I use an aerial silk swing attached to the chin up bar in my home, other options include:

- characters can use a swing at a playground
- characters can sway side-to-side while standing
- characters can perform arm circles or swing their hands up and

down and/or side to side
- characters can mimic swinging in another way, such as, alternating between balancing on their heels then their foot pads

9. Wading/Floating (unorthodox)

This technique has a similar function as swinging and swaying techniques, in that it can soothe the nervous system, simulate a nurturing action, possibly psychologically recreate amniotic-type sensations, and gently move the body to stimulate the SNS. All of these can bring the character back into regulation. Characters can visit a professional float centre or public swimming pool. However, since that can be hard to arrange when someone is triggered in real-life (and you want to remain as accurate and authentic as possible in your trauma-informed fiction), a home bath, spa, or pool might be better for the character/s.

Like the techniques outlined under the hyperarousal/hypervigilance subheading, this is only a portion of choices available to your characters. Feel free to write any notes or thoughts that came up as you read through this list. You might like to refer to these notes while completing the upcoming questions and exercises.

Matching Character Preferences to Techniques

Again, I have made the occasional allusion to good therapy matches for certain characters throughout the above techniques (so you might want to have another read through). Here are some more ideas:
- bibliotherapy for book lovers
- art therapy for the creatives (or, perhaps, a character who had their artistic talents stifled by social or parental expectations?)
- green therapy for nature-loving characters

For Sieg, since he is an ex-runner, he might have an affinity for the great outdoors, hence, green therapy could be another option for him. Did you find anything in the list that might appeal to your character?

Questions and Exercises

If you have chosen a mostly hypoaroused character, what are some of the techniques described in this chapter that you might like to incorporate in your character therapy sessions and plot? Think about:

- your own interests
- the interests of your traumatised character (match their preferences)
- what you think you could portray
- whether it seems like a logical and intuitive recovery choice for the character, plot, and trauma arc
- do you need to carry out more research on your chosen recovery interventions?

Chapter 19 – Short-Term Techniques for Post-Trauma Effects in Your Characters, Part 3

In real-life, a client (and even a therapist) may not fully understand whether the presenting symptomology is on the hypoaroused or hyperaroused spectrum. Indeed, the symptoms may be a combination of the two, as I have shown with Sieg. This chapter deals with techniques that can be used by any of your characters, which helps if you too are unsure of what techniques to choose. Some of the following techniques have been adapted from other theorists and experts. I do not claim sole creation of *all* of them. Like the recommendation given in the hyperaroused and hypoaroused chapters, please receive expert clearance and support if you choose to test any of these techniques for yourself.

Techniques for Both Types of Triggered Effects

Some suggested techniques that can be used by your traumatised character for any type of post-trauma effect when triggered in the short-term (and for 'first-aid') are:

1. Any movement, but especially rocking and shaking (unorthodox)
   The reasons for this should be obvious based on previous information provided, namely, they can help to soothe, comfort, and settle the nervous system.

1A. This is a technique I call 'Shake it off' (unorthodox)
   As soon as it is safe to do so, have the character move, shake their hands/feet/body, and/or rock to aid the nervous system in dispersing traumatic energy. The shake-it-off technique can be added into a longer recovery process.

1B. I call this the 'Rocking foetal position' (unorthodox)
   Get the character to sit down and bend their knees. Have them rest their chin or face against their knees and wrap their arms around their shins.

They then rock gently for a count of ten. Then, lie them down on their left side (this is important because it is the side the heart is on). Get them to bring their knees up to their chest. Wrap their arms around their shins. Rest their chin or face against their knees. Rock gently for a count of ten. Change to the right side. Have the character repeat as above. Return to the seated rocking foetal position and rock gently for a count of ten.

2. Create and play with what I call a 'Comfort toy box' (unorthodox)

I have adapted this exercise from the common 'Dialectical Behavioural Therapy' (DBT) 'comfort box' practice. The comfort toy box does not have to be a literal box, it can be playful objects that you scatter around the house. However, it can also be a literal box, such as a shoe box or plastic container. Or, it can be both. I have both. Get your character to source toys (yes, toys) which bring them comfort. Specifically, think of the toys in their childhood which brought them comfort and, if they no longer own them, have the character seek them out to fill up their box and/or scatter around their home. Think about whether there were any toys they were *not* allowed to play with. Have the character source them. The character can bring out their comfort box every day, whether they feel dysregulated or not, to increase feelings of comfort and safety (and play) into their daily life. Several ideas for toys your character can add to their comfort toy box are:

- toy cars
- yoyos
- mini Barbie playsets or full-sized Barbies
- spinning tops
- fidget toys
- Lego
- wooden blocks
- paper dolls
- toy trains

Other ways to incorporate/adjust this technique include:
- placing a favourite teddy bear at the end of their bed
- putting a favourite childhood movie in easy view of the television,

to encourage rewatching and/or to incite happy memories upon seeing the movie displayed.

- getting some posters of things they loved as a child and putting them up on their walls.

Because the comfort toy box is a daily activity, it can become part of the long-term recovery plan.

3. Listening to classical, relaxing, or meditation music; anything calm and relaxing, even lullabies (unorthodox)

These types of music can aid in calming the nervous system. The music can play in the therapist's office and/or your character can be encouraged to blast their favourite music (which might be uptempo), when triggered.

4. Self-hugs (both)

There are many variations of this exercise. You might like to have your character try this one:

- place the left palm on right shoulder and the right palm over the left shoulder.
- alternate a patting motion, one shoulder, then the other for several, slow beats (the slow movement is especially important if the heart rate is increased as in a hyperaroused response)
- stop the patting but keep the hands on the shoulders, then begin a slow rocking motion. Perform the rocking in any way which feels soothing.
- adding a 'shhhh' sound to the rocking can also prove beneficial
- adding a mantra can also help. Pick something such as 'I am worthy of love'.

Self-hugs can form part of the long-term recovery process.

5. Safe place (both)

This technique requires caution, since having a person 'get into their head' soon after trauma can make matters worse. The same goes for meditation practices, as noted by David A. Treleaven's research in this area. Even so, it can prove effective when survivors do not feel safe anywhere.

To complete, have the character close their eyes or leave them open (whichever feels safest). Next, get them to imagine a place where they feel safe (an isolated beach? A log cabin? A bright forest with a bunch of baby animals surrounding them? The ocean on a houseboat? A deserted island with a warm lagoon at the centre? A specific house? A fairy tale world? It can be anywhere, real or fictional). Then, they can create the world using all the senses until it feels real. Get the character to 'go' to this place in their minds when they feel triggered. Alternatively, consider incorporating this technique into part of a fantasy or surrealist sequence in your book. This can also become part of the long-term recovery plan.

6. Grounding (both)

Again, there are a variety of grounding exercises. Here is one of mine:

- the character should go somewhere that has grass and/or dirt (their front or back gardens are fine)
- take their shoes off
- stand on the grass/dirt in bare feet
- close or keep their eyes open according to what feels safe
- take three slow breaths in and out
- have the character focus on the feelings and sensations in/on/around their feet
- imagine a light coming out of the soles of their feet, shooting deep into the earth, keeping them safely connected to the world
- take three slow breaths in and out to finish
- open their eyes (if they were closed).

Grounding is another good option to include in the long-term recovery plan.

7. Sigh it away (unorthodox)

When faced with a difficult situation, sighing can briefly disrupt an automatic/triggered trauma response. Different types of sighs have been shown to help different people, so you might like to experiment with this one—when you are untriggered, and when you have been medically and psychologically cleared to do it — so you know which ones would work best for your characters. You could try deep sighs versus shallow sighs, loud ones versus soft ones, and those voiced through the mouth versus the nose.

Again, these are only a handful of accepted techniques you can draw upon to depict in your novel for short-term application by your character/s when triggered post-trauma. There are many more options as well as long-term techniques to consider. One option for the long-term recovery process is detailed in the next couple of chapters.

Matching Character Preferences to Techniques

The comfort toy box technique is the most obvious character-matching example provided in this section. A couple of extra examples include:
- an opera lover listening to classical music
- self-hugs for those characters in need of physical touch and self-love
- safe place technique for characters with a good imagination

Returning to Sieg as an example, we might want to incorporate the safe place technique for him, seeing as he is having a hard time feeling safe at work. What do you think? Did any of the techniques inspire your own imagination? Were there any you had not thought of? What 'called' to your characters? Let the muse take you to the questions and answers section now.

Questions and Exercises

What are some of the techniques described in this chapter that you might like to incorporate in your character therapy sessions and plot? Think about:
- your own interests
- the interests of your traumatised character (match their preferences)
- what you think you could portray
- whether it seems like a logical and intuitive recovery choice for the character, plot, and trauma arc
- do you need to carry out more research on your chosen recovery interventions?

Chapter 20 – A Long-Term Intervention, Part 1

Multiple 'positive recovery processes' and 'positive paths to recovery' exist. Through my research, I refined a theoretically backed process which I termed the '3SPRP', or 'the 3-step positive recovery process', adapted from existing theories. Regardless of the chosen process or path, the goal remains the same for all of them, namely, a method for positive, long-term recovery. Recovery in this context refers to a trauma survivor being able to manage post-trauma effects, move into the post-trauma stage of their lives with resilience, post-traumatic growth, and an increased window of tolerance, and limit the potential for triggers.

Despite developing, and advocating for, the 3SPRP, I agree with Judith Lewis Herman, who says 'recovery is never complete'. Trauma survivors do not magically wake up one day, even after following a positive recovery process, and think 'I am healed!'. Recovery from trauma is an ongoing, often lifelong, spiral-like experience. Even so, processes, like the 3SPRP, have been shown in the research to assist trauma survivors in the long-term. Whichever long-term approach you choose to represent in your novel, ensure it is backed by research. If you choose not to follow the process I detail below, I highly recommend reading the research of other experts, especially Judith Lewis Herman.

As the name of my process suggests, there are three (not necessarily linear) steps which make up the 3 Step Positive Recovery Process, these being:

1. **Safety:** Increase the trauma survivor's sense of safety
2. **Re-embodying:** re-embody the trauma survivor (i.e. increase the awareness of their body, sensations, feelings)
3. **Reconnecting:** reconnect the trauma survivor to their life, identity, and others post-trauma.

Having a fundamental understanding of the steps which make up this process will help, as will knowing ways to represent each step. Since it is essential to grasp each stage of the 3SPRP, a chapter is devoted to each part, starting with a discussion on 'safety' in this chapter.

What is Safety?

Drawing on the work of a variety of theorists, I define a sense of safety as the feeling of control over one's body, one's life, and one's relationships. Since trauma, as I have defined it throughout this book, refers to an experience/s which threatens feelings of safety and subsequent ideas of the self, this aspect of the recovery journey takes on a new dimension. Indeed, it can be, and has been, argued to be the most important part. As such, you will need to zoom in on this aspect of the long-term journey in your story.

How to Represent a Character Experiencing Safety

Multiple suggestions are offered below, with a note in brackets as to whether these would be classed as orthodox, unorthodox, or both, therapies. Some of these suggestions may be relevant to your story and some may not. You will have to decide that. I have again used the bank robbery example to offer a more specific view of each suggestion to assist you:

1. Surround the character with a positive support system (both)

    This can be in the form of friends, family, mental health workers, or even colleagues. Anyone who supports the person on their recovery journey and helps them to feel safe with them. In case I need to make the obvious clear: one of the support people should be the love interest if you are writing a romance subgenre. It can also mean the main character may need to exclude people from their lives post-trauma. As mentioned, this is a common occurrence for trauma survivors.

    Examples: You could show Sieg being offered time off and free therapy paid for by the bank. He could have a best friend who steps up and offers to stay with him since he lives alone and is triggered when he is alone (perhaps Sieg was isolated from the other hostages during his ordeal?)

2. Provide the character with as much control over their body as possible (both)

    Have other characters ask permission before touching, hugging, performing medical interventions, etc. on the traumatised character. Doing this gives a trauma survivor a sense of control and power over themselves and their lives, even if it is within a limited context. Starting small in this way opens avenues for a greater experience of control and power in their lives. Get a professional (therapist, counsellor, mental health worker, nurse, doctor, etc.) to explain to other characters the importance of asking before doing.

Example: Since Sieg was grabbed and held hostage with a knife at his throat, this step is likely going to be important. At the hospital afterwards, you could show the nurses and doctors asking before touching his wounds. Many hospital staff are trauma-informed these days, so this would not be unusual.

3. Provide the character with as much control over their life as possible (both)

Again, have other characters ask the traumatised character what they want. Give the character choices (especially if the character is in a hypoaroused state. In this state, trauma survivors might not know what they want or need. Asking may help shake up their decision-making pathways). This is for the same reasons offered at number 2.

Example: Go back and review the sample session I provided for Sieg. You will see the choices the therapist offered him. Though they might seem small (e.g., giving him the choice of where to sit), these small choices can make a huge impact on trauma survivors.

4. Provide the character with the tools necessary to differentiate between safety and danger (both)

Since trauma can disrupt the natural warning and safety systems in the BBANS, this is an important part of the safety step for long-term recovery. This issue can be dealt with in therapy sessions, where the counsellor explains non-traumatised danger and safety signals. For instance, hypervigilance can make a trauma survivor over-alert for cues (which can lead to them seeing everything as a threat), whereas hypovigilance can do the opposite (which can make a survivor prone to dangerous situations, and more trauma, since they cannot pick up danger cues and react too slowly to threats). Therapists can discuss healthy relationship behaviours, boundaries, wants/needs, danger cues, safety signals, and personal rights to help the character re-establish a functional warning-safety system.

Example: In the sample session provided, Sieg displays several hyperaroused signs. Therefore, the therapist may decide to look at helping Sieg downplay this over-reactive response in their future sessions. Some of the ways this could be done include explaining the reasons for Sieg's hypervigilance to him, assuring him this is a normal response to a traumatic event, discussing the symptoms and the effect it has on him/his life, continuing to create a safe space for him to eventually relax his hyperarousal symptoms, and through specific therapeutic interventions (such as those discussed throughout the short-term technique chapters). Likewise, Sieg also displayed hypoaroused symptoms in the therapy session, such as avoidance. By avoiding his disturbing thoughts and feelings, this can limit his ability to fully know his wants and needs and, as a consequence, can interfere with forming healthy boundaries (and impact his relationships, but we will get to that part of trauma more thoroughly in upcoming chapters).

5. Journalling (unorthodox)

Writing in a journal can provide a private, safe space through which to explore complicated emotions. It also gives the trauma survivor a sense of control over their narrative, which can be particularly good for those characters who are resistant to traditional therapeutic methods. This is a form of scriptotherapy.

Example: The therapist could ask Sieg to note down any time he feels especially on high alert or wanting to avoid his thoughts. This can help both Sieg and the therapist to identify patterns around his triggered moments and avoidance issues.

6. Animal therapy (unorthodox)

Bessel van der Kolk notes how 'when adults or children are too ... shut down to derive comfort from human beings, relationships with other mammals can help'. Therefore, if you would like to have a subplot with a support animal such as a dog or horse, this is backed by research.

Hypovigilant characters could be especially great candidates for this form of therapy, but it is an option for all.

Example: If the therapist discovered that Sieg used to ride horses as a child, they might suggest equine therapy as a way for him to reclaim his former trust in the world and those around him.

7. Other ways (both)

Have the character perform small, daily tasks which increase a feeling of safety in both the home and outside worlds (and in themselves). Interactions between the traumatised character and intended support people, especially any romantic love interest/s, should also assist in creating a sense of safety in their internal life. Positive interactions with support people can develop a sense of internal safety which can grow into the external world.

Example: Sieg's continued positive interactions with the therapist, as well as anyone else important to his recovery process, should help with the latter. For the former suggestion, the therapist, or a friend, might encourage Sieg to get out and about, such as doing the grocery shopping. I used this technique in *The Love Healer* when I had Neoma's best friend leave her notes with small errand requests written on them.

8. Other ways (unorthodox)

Get the traumatised character to watch uplifting movies, listen to uplifting music, read uplifting books (to serve as a form of 'bibliotherapy'). Additionally, you could use the 'safe place' technique and the 'comfort toy box' techniques mentioned in the previous chapter.

Example: Since Sieg likes horses, perhaps a horse-themed movie would make a good choice for him? Maybe the therapist could prescribe a horse-themed book? Sieg could also add some horse figurines into a comfort toy box.

Like initial trauma responses, the 3SPRP is not necessarily a linear trauma recovery process. Thus, safety step exercises can be carried out at the same time as exercises for the other two steps: re-embodying and reconnection. Re-embodying is discussed in the next chapter.

Matching Character Preferences to Techniques

Once more, these techniques can/should also be matched to the character's preferences. The examples I provided with Sieg under each technique shows how to do this.

Questions and Exercises

1. In what ways will you show your character experiencing safety on their recovery journey?
2. Who will be involved? (e.g., therapist, friends, neighbours, colleagues, family, other)
3. How can you match the technique to your character's preferences?

Chapter 21 – A Long-Term Intervention Part 2

Note: As per the previous chapters, the techniques in this chapter are followed by brackets containing the words 'orthodox', 'unorthodox', or 'both' to show which therapy the technique aligns with the best. These distinctions can help you in the choices you make based on your character's main trauma therapy. This chapter will now turn to a discussion on what I call 're-embodying'.

What is Re-Embodying?

During a traumatic experience, trauma response can shut down the feelings and sensations of an individual's body (to keep the individual safe). As a result, sometimes the body remains numb after the event is over (as a post-trauma effect). This is especially true for trauma survivors experiencing hypoarousal effects (but it is still sometimes evident in the hyperaroused). Therefore, establishing the ability to recognise feelings and sensations in the body is important for long-term recovery. This is my definition of re-embodying, but what do other theorists say on the matter?

Despite using different terminology, Anna Ferguson refers to this step as 'building body awareness' and defines it as when a trauma survivor directs their attention onto their bodily experiences, sensations, and movements. Bessel van der Kolk discusses the importance of 'awareness of our ... body-based feelings' and Pete Walker advocates for 'getting out of your head and into your body' by feeling the body's feelings. My definition, therefore, corresponds well with these experts through the focus on feelings and sensations in the body. This is something to show: your characters learning, or being taught, as part of the trauma arc.

How to Represent a Character Re-Embodying

Since, primarily, this step is about getting the character back in touch with their body and bodily sensations, in theory, any activity which encourages this action can technically be depicted. Even so, there are some specific research-backed activities, techniques, and methods which you can use for your characters to show them re-embodying. Some examples are offered below, with a note in brackets as to whether these would be classed as orthodox, unorthodox, or both therapies:

1. The VSS (unorthodox)

   This acronym stands for the Vital Signs Scan. The VSS is an idea for a body-based unorthodox therapeutic tool that I developed based on a combination of existing techniques that I explored throughout my research. The VSS is completed by performing a mental scan of the body to check in with three of the four main vital signs: heart rate, breathing, and body temperature.

   How your character can perform the VSS: have the character focus their attention, one at a time, on their heart rate, breathing, and body temperature. Get the character to consider how these vital signs 'feel' to them. Is their heart rate steady, strong, fast, weak? Does their breathing seem shallow, fast, deep, slow? What about their body temperature (too hot, too cold, just right)? Regardless of whether these 'feel' within a normal range, the focused attention is meant to shift the individual into an awareness of their physical body, bring their 'logical brain' (the pre-frontal cortex) online and, as a result, calm the triggered nervous system and body.

Due to its focus on the body's subjective feelings, the VSS complies with body-based and somatic psychological theories, such as those supported by Bessel van Der Kolk, Peter Levine, and Pat Ogden. The technique was also based on a more traditional 'body scan' mixed with the body awareness techniques promoted by the above unorthodox therapists. A traditional body scan is another option (detailed next).

2. Traditional body scan (both)

   Once again, there are multiple variations to this scan, with mine as follows:
   - close or keep the eyes open according to feelings of safety
   - start at the feet and notice any feelings, sensations, or tingles
   - move up the body, noticing the different sensations, until the head is reached
   - open eyes if they have been closed

3. Dance (unorthodox)

> Any form of dance is fine. However, for female characters in particular, I personally recommend belly-dancing. I practice the Egyptian Raqs Sharqi and Moroccan Shikhat forms. Belly dance helped me not only to get in touch with my ancestral roots (Moroccan), but also in re-embodying after my own complex trauma experiences. Some research has also been carried out on the benefits of dance in re-embodying trauma survivors, so my experience is not purely anecdotal in this instance. Get your character up on their feet and swaying to the beat!

4. Meditation (both)

> Though I have mentioned this briefly, meditation techniques come with a warning. Research carried out by David A. Treleaven has shown that, especially in the early stages of trauma recovery, meditation can exacerbate post-trauma effects. Anecdotally, I experienced this disturbing exacerbation myself — and I have been meditating and performing relaxation exercises since I was four years old. Hence, I can vouch for the possibility of meditation worsening post-trauma effects. Be careful with this one (both for yourself and your character). As an aside, now I am many years into my positive recovery process, meditation has become beneficial again.
>
> Examples for your character: you could use meditation as a plot point in some interesting ways, such as showing the character having flashbacks during their meditation practice. Or, showing positive effects once they are further along their path.

4A. Mindfulness (both)

> Alongside meditation are the plethora of mindfulness practices available to your characters. These are less likely to result in negative and unwanted effects, so you might like to portray your character starting with one of these practices first.
>
> Example: when it comes to Sieg, the therapist could suggest he practices mindful walking each day. This could assist in calming his over-active thoughts and offering an exercise-related outlet to burn off some of his excess energy.

5. Yoga (unorthodox)

This is another therapeutic intervention researched by Bessel van der Kolk. Pick any type of yoga your character is likely to prefer, so long as the focus is on being conscious of the body and breath. Remember, the point of this step is to *re-embody*. Characters need to 'get back into their bodies' and become aware of their bodily feelings and sensations. If that means your character needs to sweat it out in a Bikram Yoga program, have at it.

6. Martial Arts (unorthodox)

Warning: Martial arts can cause distress for women who have experienced male-based violence since most martial arts classes have a higher proportion of men to women. If you would like to include martial arts in your story, you can overcome any potential retraumatisation in your character by ensuring it is represented as a women-specific class, or have a traumatised female character engage in a one-on-one class (with a potential love interest? This is the path I took in *See Her Run*). Alternatively, you could have a female-led class. Otherwise, a bunch of the female traumatised character's friends could come along to the class for support. Some of the martial arts mentioned by Besse van der Kolk as possible choices are:

- Aikido
- Judo
- Tae Kwon Do
- Kendo
- Jiu Jitsu
- Capoeira

Capoeira is an especially intriguing choice since it incorporates dance-type elements into the techniques. Therefore, survivors can, theoretically, receive benefits from both 'dance' and martial arts at the same time. You could also have your character decide to study a martial art from their cultural or ethnic background. For example, a Korean character might prefer Tae Kwon Do, a Japanese character might like Karate, and a Brazilian character could show an interest in Brazilian Jiu Jitsu.

7. Movement (unorthodox)

   Most forms of movement can be beneficial in re-embodying, so long as they are done with conscious intention and the character (and therapist teaching the technique) centres awareness of sensations and feelings throughout the chosen movements.

8. Breathing (both)

   An example is the 'mindful slow breathing' technique mentioned in chapter 17, page 115. Of course, dozens of other breathing exercises can be taught to your character, this is simply one option.

9. 9. Other ways (unorthodox)

   Some of the techniques mentioned in chapters 17–19, including shake it off, self-hugs, grounding, progressive muscle relaxation, swinging, and dead hangs can be employed. Another technique is stretching to the point where the character can notice it (but not to the point of harm). Characters might also want to experiment with different forms of stretching, such as active and dynamic stretches.

   Like the safety step, the re-embodying step can be carried out at the same time as the reconnection step, detailed in the next chapter.

Matching Character Preferences to Techniques

Like the previous chapter, examples have been given under each technique. Use these examples as guidance for applying them to your own characters. As usual, consider your character's background, preferences, and personal experiences when deciding.

Questions and Exercises

1. In what ways will you show your character re-embodying on their recovery journey?
2. Who will be involved? (e.g., therapist, friends, neighbours, colleagues, family, other)
3. How can you match the technique to your character's preferences?

Chapter 22 - Reconnection

Reconnection is probably the most neglected part of a trauma recovery journey. This could be because relationships are deeply impacted by a trauma survivor's post-trauma symptomology and behaviours. Arguably, it is this deep impact which makes reconnection a necessary, even if difficult, step.

What is Reconnection?

Judith Lewis Herman defines reconnecting with others as a trauma survivor having 'regained the ability to feel autonomous while remaining connected to others'. Sarah Woodhouse notes how 'moving past trauma always involves reconnection' and Deb Dana asserts that 'we never lose the need and the longing to be safely connected to others'. Anna Ferguson describes reconnection as reclaiming 'trust in yourself and others' and 'your environment' and Marie Crowe includes a sense of control over one's life and identity as important in the recovery process.

As such, I define reconnection as the attempts made to re-establish connections between the trauma survivor and their life, identity, and those around them/ others post-trauma. This definition corresponds with the opinions of these other theorists through the focus on self, life, identity, and other people. The inclusion of 'identity' is important in this definition since it is well-established in the research literature that a trauma survivor will need to develop a new identity post-trauma.

How to Represent a Character Reconnecting

Suggested techniques are offered below, with a note in brackets as to whether these would be classed as reconnection to the self, life, identity, or others as well as whether they are orthodox, unorthodox, or both types of therapy.

1. Performing activities the character used to enjoy (life and identity) (both)

   Can include hobbies, leisure activities, and exercise. Doing so reconnects them into their life by showing them how enjoyable it can be, and can help to establish a new post-trauma identity.

2. Engaging in simple, daily activities and chores (life) (both)

    This technique helps the trauma survivor reconnect with the responsibilities of life. Several examples include:
    - making the bed
    - washing dishes/packing the dishwasher
    - vacuuming
    - paying bills
    - doing the laundry

3. Meeting new people (others) (both)

    This can help when the survivor is further along in their recovery journey. It is **not** something that should be attempted immediately (unless the new person is a love interest/s).

4. Getting out into the world (life) (both)

    Again, slowly does it with this one. Too much, too soon can backfire. The point is to get your character enthusiastic about reconnecting to the possibilities of their life. You could:
    - have the character return to work on a part-time basis
    - have the character return to part-time study
    - have the character go grocery shopping (not online shopping)

5. Trying new things (life and identity) (both)

    This can give the traumatised character a sense of accomplishment, build self-trust, help them reconnect with their life via the 'shine of the new', and establish their post-trauma identity. It can also expand their window of tolerance.

6. Self-care activities (self and identity) (unorthodox)

    Self-care is another one of those fad terms which, via an increase in popular awareness, has led to a watering down and misunderstanding of its meaning. At its most basic, self-care refers to activities which care for an individual's physical, mental, emotional, sexual, and psychological health. For instance:

- regular exercise
- meditation (with the previous warning considered)
- bathing
- grooming
- eating nutritious meals at regular intervals
- getting enough rest and sleep
- being firm with sexual boundaries

7. Going out with friends (others) (both)

   Get the traumatised character and friend/s to do the activities they used to do together, before the trauma changed their relationship. This is one way the traumatised character can reconnect with others again.

8. Positive touch experiences (self and others) (both)

   This might be an excellent form of therapy for those traumas which involved a physical or sexual violence element. Have the traumatised character (slowly, and only if they have consented) receive positive touch experiences, such as:

   - massage
   - hugs
   - hairbrushing (by someone else)
   - hand-holding
   - gentle pats and/or strokes on non-sexual body parts
   - fist bumps
   - manicure and/or pedicure
   - hair cut with scalp massage

9. Other techniques (orthodox)

   The cognitive reframing technique mentioned in chapter 17 could be a good alternative technique. It can help reconnect a survivor to their new post-trauma identity.

The above techniques are only a sample of the possibilities available to survivors undertaking the 3SPRP or other types of positive recovery paths or processes.

Use the examples provided as fluid guidelines rather than set rules. The field of trauma theory expands every day, especially when it comes to the unorthodox, so do not get too fixated on the right/best therapy. Remember, the best therapy is the one that works (in the immediate, short-term, and long-term) and you are the expert when it comes to your character.

Matching Character Preferences to Techniques

Looking over the provided techniques, did anything jump out at you? Do any of the techniques align with something your character is interested in, or has a connection to in their past? Could you add something to their backstory to correspond to these techniques?

Questions and Exercises

1. In what ways will you show your character reconnecting on their recovery journey?
2. Who will be involved? (e.g., therapist, friends, neighbours, colleagues, family, other)
3. How can you match the technique to your character's preferences?

Chapter 23 - Bringing it All Together

Final Checks

Once you have a full outline or first draft, the first check is to ensure you have met your main fiction genre's expectations and conventions. What tropes, characters, common plot devices, and endings are you supposed to have in your book? Did you include everything? Fix it up now.

Secondly, go back and check you have included the necessary trauma elements for your chosen trauma-themed subgenre in your fiction. Are they all there? Most importantly: at a minimum, have you represented the traumatic event or experience? If not, add it.

Next, check your arcs. In chapter 4 of this book, I noted the three arcs your trauma-themed subgenre fiction may need to incorporate, namely, the character arc, the trauma arc, and the relationship arc. If you have not addressed them, now is the time. If your trauma survivor does not go through an explicit trauma recovery process — for instance, if that is not a requirement of your chosen subgenre — they still (probably) need to have a happy ending.

Completing the trauma arc will be easier to achieve in the post-trauma subgenres because representing the trauma, its effects, and positive post-trauma recovery attempts forms the necessary features of the subgenre. For the other trauma-themed subgenres, think about a beginning, middle, and end. The beginning is the trauma; the middle shows whether this impacted the survivor in a minor way or not (this will change according to the specific trauma-themed subgenre); the end is not letting the trauma interfere in the character's life long-term. Have a think about how you can achieve this now if you have not already.

To finish the character arc, you again need to consider a beginning, middle, and end. Ponder the following: who was the character pre-trauma? How did the trauma change them? How does interacting with the love interest/s and/ or other plot elements help the character who experienced trauma to change, mature, and grow?

The relationship arc depends on who you choose to include in it. Is it romantic, non-romantic, both, or none? Ensure you have finalised each relationship arc you started.

Finally, have you represented each trauma element as authentically, accurately, and sensitively as possible? Did you use the suggestions offered throughout this book? Did you also apply your own research? Have you ensured you are as close to the accepted research as possible? Did you avoid victim blaming and shaming? As much as possible, did you stick to the facts and the research? If you have done all of this, your final checks are complete, and your manuscript is ready to rewrite to first draft or final draft stage.

Into the Future of Trauma-Themed Subgenres

Although this book overviewed the current, research-backed ways to write trauma, trauma responses, post-trauma effects, and post-trauma recovery, it is still only **one** way to write about these significant topics within the trauma-themed subgenres. Trauma theory changes all the time. Here are a couple of my personal predictions around changes in trauma theory and trauma writing to look out for in the future:

- more trauma-themed subgenres will come to light, with their own associated definitions and features
- there will be a shift in real-life towards the more unorthodox methods, which will need to translate into fictional representation
- more definitive definitions of trauma, trauma response, and post-trauma effects will occur
- new immediate techniques to prevent post-trauma effects will be discovered
- I also hope that, one day, there will no longer be a need for the trauma genre or trauma-themed subgenres because we will learn to stop traumatising each other

Goodbye From Me

You made it! Thank you for following me on what I know can be a difficult (but also rewarding) writing path. You should feel proud of yourself for coming this far. Good luck in continuing your personal trauma-informed writer's journey!

All the best,
Dr A.K. Leigh
www.yourromancebookdoctor.com
www.fallinlovewithleigh.com

Glossary

3SPRP = an acronym which stands for the 3 Step Positive Recovery Process. It involves safety (increasing the trauma survivor's sense of safety), re-embodying (increasing the trauma survivor's awareness of their body, sensations, and feelings), and reconnecting (reconnecting the trauma survivor to their life and identity post-trauma).

8FTRM = an acronym which stands for the 8F Trauma Response Model. A theoretical model which details eight possible trauma responses starting with F in English: flood, freeze, flight, fawn, fight, fright, flag, and faint.

9FTRM = an acronym which stands for the 9F Trauma Response Model. A theoretical model which details nine possible trauma responses starting with F in English: flood, freeze, flight, fawn, fight, fright, flag, faint, and fade.

Art Therapy = using art as a therapeutic tool.

Background Trauma Fiction = a novel which contains a brief mention of a past or present trauma but does not include a representation or depiction of the trauma.

BBANS = an acronym which stands for Brain, Body, And Nervous System. It refers to the interconnectedness of the brain, body, and nervous system in trauma response.

Bibliotherapist = a professional therapist who 'prescribes' books/reading for therapeutic use.

Bibliotherapy = using reading as a therapeutic tool.

Body-Based Therapies = using the body to treat post-trauma effects.

Book Prescription = a book suggested by a bibliotherapist to assist in therapeutic recovery.

Bottom-Up Approach = using the body to aid in regulating post-trauma effects occurring in the brain, namely, you use the body (bottom) to regulate the brain (up). Also see *Body-Based Therapies*.

CBT = Cognitive Behavioural Therapy.

Cognitive Reframing = when a negative or unhelpful thought, idea, emotion, or feeling is identified, then consciously replaced (i.e., 'reframed') in a positive and helpful way.

Cognitive Restructuring = see *Cognitive Reframing.*

Comorbid/Comorbidity = a symptom, disease, or disorder that commonly appears alongside other symptoms, diseases, and disorders.

Coping Mechanism = the (mostly) conscious strategies used by trauma survivors to help them cope with the lasting effects of trauma. Tend to manifest in physical form.

CPTSD/CPTSR = an acronym which stands for Complex Post-Traumatic Stress Disorder/ Complex Post-Traumatic Stress Reaction. Post-trauma symptoms related to this condition commonly present after multiple, prolonged, inescapable, repeated, or long-term (chronic) traumatic events.

Default Mode = see *Lingering Mode.*

Defence Mechanism = the (mostly) unconscious strategies used by trauma survivors to protect, repress, or defend against the lasting effects of trauma. Tend to manifest in mental and emotional form.

Depersonalise/Depersonalisation = feeling detached from the self/body, as if watching yourself outside of the body.

Derealise/Derealisation = feeling as if the world and/or yourself, or part of your experience, is not real.

Dissociate/Dissociation = loss of awareness of present surroundings; blacking out; an attempt by the BBANS to forget disturbing memories.

EMDR = an acronym which stands for Eye Movement Desensitisation and Reprocessing. An unorthodox trauma recovery technique using specific eye movements to rewire the brain, thereby impacting post-trauma effects.

Eustress = a type of beneficial stress for the BBANS.

Fade = a FAST response which refers to attempts at, or the wish to, hide, 'fade into the background', and/or disappear.

Faint = a FAST response recognisable by dizziness, fuzzy-headedness, falling asleep, and/or fainting to limit possible pain perception in a human being.

FAST = an acronym which stands for Fear, Anxiety, Stress, and Trauma. It refers to the most common reactions an individual will have to a threatening situation. Whether the situation results in fear, anxiety, stress, or trauma depends on a multitude of factors, including (but not limited to) a sense of the level of threat, length of threat, outcome of the threat, how the person's identity/sense of self was affected, and even previous exposure to threats.

Fawn = a FAST response noted when an individual attempts to placate, appease, or submit to stop and/or prevent a perceived threat.

Fight = a FAST response which refers to the urge to verbally and/or physically fight a perceived threat.

Flag = a FAST response recognisable when an individual 'shuts down' physically, mentally, and emotionally to limit possible pain perception.

Flight = a FAST response which involves running away, fleeing, or trying to escape a threatening situation.

Flood = a FAST response caused when a potential threat is recognised, so the individual is flooded by powerful emotions.

Freeze = a FAST response identified by an individual stopping or limiting movement or being on guard/watchful/alert so they can gather information for their next steps and to prevent the likelihood of being spotted.

Fright = a FAST response noted when an individual feels unable to move (also known as 'tonic immobility') and/or plays dead.

Green Therapy = see *Nature Therapy*.

Guilt = the negative feelings we have of ourselves based on something we have done (or perceive we have done).

HEA = an acronym which stands for Happily-Ever-After. Typically, this is when a story ends with a couple being married or engaged.

HFN = an acronym which stands for Happy-For-Now. This more modern version of a HEA is when a story ends with a couple deciding to get back together, stay in a relationship, or live together.

Hypervigilance/Hyperarousal = defined by physiological adaptations, behaviours, and symptoms which align with the lingering flood, freeze, flight, fight, fright, fawn, and fade trauma responses.

Hypovigilance/Hypoarousal = defined by physiological adaptations, behaviours, and symptoms which align with the lingering fright, faint, and flag trauma responses.

Initial Trauma Response = the automatic response (or responses) to a traumatic event as it is happening. Also known as the 'trauma reaction'. These responses lead to specific physiological, biological, emotional, and neurological behaviours and symptoms designed to bring the human being through the threatening experience alive and safe.

Lingering Mode = when the initial trauma responses linger and evolve into post-trauma effects which mimic the symptoms and behaviours experienced during the traumatic event if the trauma survivor is 'triggered'.

Literary Method = the techniques used to represent trauma in the way a book is written.

Micro Skills = the foundational tools used by professional therapists to elicit feelings of safety, acceptance, and being understood in the client.

Nature Therapy = using nature as a therapeutic tool.

Non-Trauma Fiction = see *Background Trauma*.

Orthodox Therapies = any interventions which maintain a top-down (or talk-based) approach, such as psychology, all talking-based therapies, CBT, and exposure therapies.

Plotting Method = the way you write characters and plot events which affect characters (such as trauma).

Post-Trauma Effects = an experience/s which threatens feelings of safety and subsequent ideas of the self (trauma) and leads to unpleasant symptoms following the experience.

Post-Trauma Romance = a work of fiction that depicts a traumatic experience/s, its post-trauma effects, and the processes of recovery from the traumatic experience/s within a romantic narrative.

Post-Trauma Subgenre = a trauma-themed subgenre which includes: trauma representation, initial trauma response/post-trauma effects, post-trauma recovery, and an impact on the romantic relationship.

PTSD/PTSR = an acronym which stands for Post-Traumatic Stress Disorder/Post-Traumatic Stress Reaction. Post-trauma symptoms related to this condition typically occur after one (sometimes more) short-term (acute) traumatic experiences.

Reconnection = attempts made to re-establish connections between the trauma survivor and their life, identity, and others.

Re-Embodying = establishing the ability to recognise feelings and sensations in the body.

Retraumatisation = a trauma survivor being exposed to situations which force them to relive their traumatic experiences. This includes *reading* and *writing* about trauma.

Romance Genre = a work of fiction that includes a love story as the central element, between two or more characters, with a happy and satisfying ending.

Safety = the feeling of control over one's body, one's life, and one's relationships.

Scriptotherapist = a professional therapist who 'prescribes' writing for therapeutic use.

Scriptotherapy = using writing as a therapeutic tool.

Secondary Trauma = see *Vicarious Trauma.*

Second-Hand Trauma = see *Vicarious Trauma.*

Shame = the negative feelings we have of ourselves based on something that has happened to us.

Talk Therapies = see *Orthodox Therapies.*

Top-Down Approach = using the brain (top) to assist in regulating trauma responses in the body (down). Also see *Orthodox Therapies.*

Tonic Immobility = see *Fright.*

Transitional Post-Trauma Romance = a work of fiction that features all of the characteristics of trauma romance and some of the characteristics of post-trauma romance.

Transitional Post-Trauma Subgenre = a trauma-themed subgenre which includes trauma representation as well as one or two of the following: initial trauma response/post-trauma effects, post-trauma recovery, and/or an impact on the romantic relationship.

Trauma = an experience/s which threatens feelings of safety and subsequent ideas of the self.

Trauma Genre = a work of fiction which incorporates an element of trauma representation into its storyline.

Trauma Reaction = see *Trauma Response.*

Trauma Recovery Journey = a series of steps which take a survivor from trauma to recovery: a traumatic event occurs (trauma), which creates a series of responses (trauma responses), that can lead to symptoms which interfere in a survivor's life (post-trauma effects and lingering trauma responses), and can lead the survivor into taking positive or negative steps towards dealing with the symptoms (post-trauma recovery attempts).

Trauma Recovery Therapies = the techniques, methods, and tools used in dealing with post-trauma effects.

Trauma Response = two main meanings, 1) the initial response (or responses) to trauma (also known as the 'trauma reaction') and 2) the possible lingering responses to trauma (i.e. post-trauma effects).

Trauma Romance = a work of fiction that depicts a traumatic experience/s within a romantic narrative.

Trauma Subgenre = a trauma-themed subgenre which includes trauma representation only.

Trauma-Themed Subgenres = Subgenres containing trauma elements. They are hybrids of a main genre (e.g. crime) and the trauma genre. See also *Trauma Genre*.

Trauma Type = there are two main types of trauma: 'one-off' (acute) and 'prolonged' (chronic).

Trigger = something that reminds an individual of the original trauma, which then sets off a series of emotional, psychological, physical, and/or physiological responses within them (usually the initial trauma response/s experienced during the original trauma).

Unorthodox Therapies = any interventions which maintain a bottom-up or non-verbal approach, such as body-movement exercises, expressive arts, and creativity.

Vicarious Trauma = when trauma is witnessed, but not personally experienced, or when trauma is spoken about via another person or source.

VSS = an acronym which stands for the Vital Signs Scan. The VSS is a body-based unorthodox therapeutic tool that I developed as part of my research. It involves performing a mental scan of the body to check in with three of the four main vital signs: heart rate, breathing, and body temperature. The individual focuses their attention, one at a time, on their heart rate, breathing, and body temperature. This aims to force the so-called logical brain online, thus over-riding the unregulated emotional brain's lingering trauma response.

Writing Prescription = a writing activity suggested by a scriptotherapist to assist in therapeutic recovery.

Recommended Reading and References

Abubakar, S. 2017, Art as narrative: recounting trauma through literature, *IRA-International Journal of Management & Social Sciences*, vol. 08, no. 01, pp. 118 –123, viewed 21 February 2022, https://pdfs.semanticscholar.org/662e/f4a811b922320f0b6002a1ffcb-1f4a115b61.pdf

American Psychiatric Association (APA). 2013, *Diagnostic and statistical manual of mental disorders V*, American Psychiatric Publishing, Washington.

Austen, J. 2014, *Pride and Prejudice*, Penguin Books, London.

Bényei, T. & Stara, A. 2014, *The edges of trauma: explorations in visual art and literature*, Cambridge Scholars Publisher, Cambridge.

Bond, L & Craps, S. 2020, *Trauma*, Routledge, Abingdon, UK.

Brontë, A. 2010, *The Tenant of Wildfell Hall,* Thomas Cautley Newby, London.

Brown, B. 2013, Shame vs. Guilt, Accessed 6 June 2023, https://brenebrown.com/articles/2013/01/15/shame-v-guilt/

Calhoun, LG. & Tedeschi, RG. (eds). 2014, *Handbook of posttraumatic growth: research and practice*, Psychology Press, New York.

Carroll, L. 2015, *Alice's adventures in Wonderland*, Barnes & Noble, Inc., New York.

Caruth, C. 2016, *Unclaimed experience: trauma, narrative, and history: twentieth anniversary edition*, John Hopkins University Press, Baltimore.

Castle, J. 2021, *Guild boss*, Piatkus Books, London.

Crowe, M. 2022, Psychiatry and/or recovery: a critical analysis, *International Journal of Mental Health Nursing*, vol. 31, pp. 1542–1551. DOI: 10.1111/inm.13072

Dana, D. 2023, *Polyvagal practices: anchoring the self in safety*, Norton Professional Books, New York.

Faulkner, W. & Gorra, M. E. 2010, *As I lay dying*, W.W. Norton, London.

Felman, S. & Laub, D. 1992, *Testimony: crises of witnessing in literature, psychoanalysis, and history*, Routledge, New York.

Ferguson, A. 2023, *The vagus nerve reset*, Penguin Life, Australia.

Fisher, J. 2021, *Transforming the living legacy of trauma: a workbook for survivors and therapists*, PESI Publishing and Media, Wisconsin.

Grabbe, L. & Miller-Karas, E. 2017, The trauma resiliency model: a "bottom-up" intervention for trauma psychotherapy, *Journal of the American Psychiatric Nurses Association*, vol. 24, no. 1, pp. 76–84. Accessed 1 November 2021, https://journals.sagepub.com/doi/abs/10.1177/1078390317745133?journalCode=japa

Herman, JL. 2022, *Trauma and recovery*, Basic Books, New York.

Hoover, C. 2016, *It ends with us*, Simon & Schuster UK Ltd., London.

Ivey, A.E, Ivey, M.B, & Zalaquett, C.P ,2014, *Intentional interviewing and counseling: facilitating client development in a multicultural society*, Brooks/Cole, Australia.

Kindleysides, A. 2024, *Broken hearts: writing the representation of trauma and trauma recovery in a post-trauma romance novel*, PhD thesis, Central Queensland

University, Brisbane, Australia. https://www.researchgate.net/publication/385565303_Broken_Hearts_Writing_The_Representation_of_Trauma_and_Trauma_Recovery_in_a_Post-Trauma_Romance_Novel_Thesis_Declaration

King, S. 2022, *Fairy tale*, Scribner, New York.

King, S. 2023, *Holly*, Scribner, New York.

Leigh, A. 2021, *The romance novel formula*, Amazon Independent Publishing, Sydney.

Leigh, A.K. 2015, *See her run*, Amazon Independent Publishing, Sydney.

Leigh, A.K. 2024, *The love healer*, Serenade Publishing, Maleny, Australia.

Levine, P. 2011, *In an unspoken voice: how the body releases trauma and restores goodness*, North Atlantic Books, Berkeley, CA.

Luckhurst, R. 2008, *The trauma question*, Routledge, London.

Malchiodi, C.A. 2005, *Expressive therapies*, Guilford Publications, New York.

Malchiodi, C.A. 2020, *Expressive arts therapy: the original psychotherapy*. Accessed 1 October 2023, https://www.psychologytoday.com/us/blog/arts-and-health/202012/expressive-arts-therapy-the-original-psychotherapy

Matz, J. 2004, *The modern novel: a short introduction*, Blackwell Publishing, Massachusetts.

McDonald, M.C. 2023, *Unbroken: the trauma response is never wrong: and other things you need to know to take back your life*, Sounds True, Boulder, Colorado.

Nestor, J. (2020), *Breath: the new science of a lost art*, Penguin Life, UK.

Ogden, P., Minton, K. & Pain, C. 2006, *Trauma and the body: a sensorimotor approach to psychotherapy*, W.W. Norton & Company, Inc., London.

Quinn, J. 2000, *The Duke and I*, Avon Books, New York.

Schauer, M. & Elbert, T. 2010, Dissociation following traumatic stress: etiology and treatment. *Journal of Psychology*, vol. 218, pp. 109–127. Accessed 1 November 2021, https://www.complextrauma.uk/uploads/2/3/9/4/23949705/dissociation_following_traumatic_stress.pdf

Schwartz, A. 2016, *The complex PTSD workbook: a mind-body approach to regaining emotional control & becoming whole*, Althea Press, California.

Shapiro, F. 2012, *Getting past your past: take control of your life with self-help techniques from EMDR therapy*, Rodale Books, New York.

Shapiro, F. 2018, *Eye movement desensitization and reprocessing (EMDR) therapy: basic principles, protocols, and procedures*, 3rd edn, The Guilford Press, New York.

Siegel, D.J. 1999, *The developing mind: toward a neurobiology of interpersonal experience*, Guilford Press, New York.

Thompson, M. 2024, *Complex PTSD: the time for healing is now*, Amazon Independent Publishing, Seattle.

Treleaven, DA 2018, *Trauma-sensitive mindfulness: practices for safe and transformative healing*, W.W. Norton & Company, New York.

Van der Kolk, B. 2001, The assessment and treatment of Complex PTSD, in R Yehuda (ed) *Traumatic stress*, pp. 1–29, American Psychiatric Press, Washington. Accessed 8 August 2022, www.researchgate.net/profile/Onno-Hart/publication/265099248_The_Assessment_and_Treatment_of_Complex_PTSD/links/545a3d1f0cf2cf5164843be5/The-Assessment-and-Treatment-of-Complex-PTSD.pdf

Van der Kolk, B. 2014, *The body keeps the score: mind, brain and body in the transformation of trauma*, Penguin Random House, New York.

Vickroy, L. 2002, *Trauma and survival in contemporary fiction*, University of Chicago Press, Chicago.

Walker, A. 2017, *The color purple*, Weidenfeld & Nicolson, London.

Walker, P. 2014, *Complex PTSD: from surviving to thriving: a guide and map for recovering from childhood trauma*, Azure Coyote Publishing, California

Wang, W., Blackburn, K.G., Thompson, R.M., Bajaj, K., Pedler, R. & Fucci, K. 2024, Trauma isn't one size fits all: how online support communities point to different diagnostic criteria for C-PTSD and PTSD, *Health Communication*, pp. 1–12. DOI: 10.1080/10410236.2024.2314343

Woodhouse, S. 2021, *You're not broken: break free from trauma & reclaim your life*, Penguin Random House, Melbourne.

Woolf, V. 1927, *To the lighthouse*, Columbia University Press, New York.

World Health Organization (WHO) n.d., *6B41 Complex post traumatic stress disorder*. Accessed 27 October 2022, https://icd.who.int/browse11/l-m/en#/http://id.who.int/icd/entity/585833559.

Acknowledgements

As usual, none of this could have been possible without the support of my amazing children. I know it isn't easy to see me 'playing on the computer' even when I call it 'working'. Thank you for understanding.

To all the trauma theorists, literary theorists, and literary trauma theorists who came before me: I could not have written this book without your foundational work. I am honoured to be following in your footsteps.

For the friends and family who stepped up and supported me during a difficult and traumatic period towards the end of my PhD: I am grateful to have you in my corner.

To my publisher, Ginninderra Press, and the wonderful Debbie Lee and Mandy Wolbers: thank you for believing in me and this book.

For my two exceptional, generous, and talented PhD supervisors — Dr Nicole Anae and Dr Jan Cattoni — I know I have said it before, but I would not have been able to complete this book if you had not taken a chance on my PhD research. I am forever grateful to you both.

To my fellow trauma-themed subgenre writers: I hope this book inspires you to write more authentic trauma elements in your work.

For all the trauma survivors: hang in there, it gets better (but it takes a while).

About Dr Alicia Leigh

Dr Leigh is an emerging trauma theorist and author of over 20 romance novels and two non-fiction writing books. Her PhD thesis — recognised as one of the 'top 10% of outstanding theses in the field' — identified the post-trauma romance subgenre and several innovative trauma theories. Her masters degree research resulted in the publication of the bestselling non-fiction title, *The Romance Novel Formula*.

She uses her postgraduate degrees in counselling and psychology to create believable, three-dimensional characters and plots. Her certificates of achievement in forensic science and forensic anthropology help her to create realistic crime elements in her stories.

When not writing, reading, teaching, editing, researching, or enjoying nature, she can be found having fun with her three gorgeous children (plus one laid back dog and one temperamental cat).

She is active on social media and encourages readers to interact with her there. Her fiction is written under the pseudonyms A.K. Leigh and Leigh Hatchmann.

Professional website
www.yourromancebookdoctor.com
Dr A.K. Leigh: Your Romance Book Doctor

Author website
www.fallinlovewithleigh.com
Fall in Love ... with Leigh